JONAH!
The Musical

DENIS O'GORMAN & BARRY HART

kevin mayhew

We hope you enjoy the music in this book. Further copies are available from your local Kevin Mayhew stockist.

In case of difficulty, or to request a catalogue, please contact the publisher direct by writing to:

The Sales Department
KEVIN MAYHEW LTD
Buxhall
Stowmarket
Suffolk IP14 3BW

Phone 01449 737978
Fax 01449 737834
E-mail info@kevinmayhewltd.com

First published in Great Britain in 1993 by Fountain Publications.
Reassigned to Kevin Mayhew Ltd. in 2003.

© Copyright 2003 Kevin Mayhew Ltd.

ISBN 1 84417 020 9
ISMN M 57024 162 0
Catalogue No: 1450268

0 1 2 3 4 5 6 7 8 9

Cover illustration by Bernard Young
Cover design by Angela Selfe
Music setter: Donald Thomson
Proof reader: Linda Ottewell

Printed and bound in Great Britain

A note about copyright in musicals

Copyright has existed for hundreds of years as a means of protecting the worth of a piece of music or text. It provides income for the composer and publisher and helps to keep the works available in print at an affordable price.

Performance Licence

Any public performance of a piece of copyright music requires a licence. Music remains protected by copyright for 70 years after the death of the composer.

Even if you do not intend to charge an entrance fee for your performance, it is necessary to apply for a licence and the minimum fee will still be payable. If you are staging more than one performance without an admission charge, you need only pay the minimum licence fee once.

If you are charging for admission, the Performance Licence will cost 10% of gross ticket sales, plus VAT, subject to the minimum fee.

The only time a performing fee is not payable is when the musical is performed within a worship service and forms part of the act of worship.

Photocopying Licence

The words and music of the songs in our musicals are protected by copyright and may not be photocopied without permission. The music may not be photocopied at all – users are expected to purchase enough copies for those performers who require the full music. The texts may be copied for learning purposes only, provided that:

- The following acknowledgement is included on each copy: © Kevin Mayhew Ltd. Used by permission from *name of musical*. Licence number......

- You pay a copyright fee of £5.85 (inc. VAT), which should be added to your performance licence cheque.

- All copies are destroyed after use.

Please note that the music and texts of our musicals are not covered by a CCL licence.

Duplicating CDs

Unfortunately we are unable to give permission for copying the accompanying CDs. It is illegal to duplicate any copyright sound recording, even for home use.

If you have any queries about copyright in Kevin Mayhew publications, please call our Copyright Department on 01449 737978.

There is a photocopiable licence application form at the back of our musicals.

Foreword

Jonah's dramatic story is given a full-scale musical treatment in this colourful retelling of the prophet's extraordinary adventure. The piece is 'through-sung' in a lively pop cantata format and the use of a choir to complement the on-stage action gives an opportunity for a large cast of youngsters to participate. There is plenty of humour and action and the music ranges from an exhilarating rock 'n' roll sequence in Nineveh to Jonah's plaintive ballad with the sea creatures inside the whale. *Jonah!* is the ideal show for schools planning a spectacular musical entertainment.

Songs

	Page
1. Jonah, can you hear me?	8

(God, Jonah, Choir)
God commands Jonah to visit the wicked city of Nineveh and preach a message of repentance. Jonah makes preparations for the journey.

2. Wait a minute, Jonah — 15
(Little Devils)
The Little Devils sow the seeds of doubt in Jonah's mind and tempt him to disobey God's instruction.

3. By Jove! you're right — 19
(Jonah, Little Devils, Choir)
Jonah runs away from the Lord and decides to catch a ship from Joppa taking him to Tarshish.

4. Jonah, I can see you — 23
(God)
Jonah is on the run, but God keeps a watchful eye on him as he attempts to make good his escape.

5. Everybody's welcome to Joppa — 25
(Holiday-makers, Workers, Comedian, Children/Choir, Spotty Kids, Granny, Sailors, Captain, Jonah)
The port of Joppa is presented as a down-at-heel seaside resort. The holiday-makers, fully kitted out for their annual treat, extol Joppa's many delights; the local children take a more jaundiced view. Jonah, after wandering in and out of the throng, is only too pleased to jump aboard a barely seaworthy vessel and head off to Tarshish as the crowd waves farewell.

6. The storm sequence — 34
(Sailors, Captain, Jonah, Choir)
The Lord sends a violent storm and the sailors call out to their gods to save them. As they throw the cargo overboard, Jonah is discovered below decks fast asleep. They pick straws to see who is to blame for the storm. Jonah gets the short straw and confesses that it is all his fault for disobeying God. He tells them to throw him overboard and, reluctantly, they agree.

7. Bye, bye, Jonah — 45
(Sailors)
The storm quietens and, standing on the side of the ship, the sailors sing a tearful farewell.

8. Underwater dance sequence 47
(God, Shoals of Fishes, Sea Horses, Crabs, Sea Creatures)
The sea creatures join in a movement sequence. The dance builds to a climax and they scatter as God calls Jonah again. They 'swim' to the side of the stage revealing Jonah's inert body lying on the sea bed.

9. Jonah, look around you 51
(God)
God sends a whale to swallow Jonah. Where elaborate staging is not possible, complete darkness with Jonah in a single spot should suggest his incarceration.

10. Yahweh, please don't leave me 55
(Jonah, Sea Creatures, Choir)
Jonah repents and, as the music broadens in the final verse, he begins to see the light and is eventually vomited onto dry land.

11. Sin city 62
(Ninevites/Choir, Little Devils)
Jonah arrives at Nineveh to find a spectacular rock 'n' roll sequence in full swing.

12. Repent! 74
(Jonah)
Dramatically, Jonah declares his message of repentance – or else!

13. Bye, bye, Jonah 77
(High Priest, Ninevites/Choir, Handmaidens)
The far from contrite Ninevites take Jonah prisoner and plan a little supper for the gods!

14. God's avenging prophet 84
(Jonah)
Breaking free, Jonah repeats his warning and exits.

15. Show him you're repenting 87
(King, Ninevites/Choir)
The king is appalled that his subjects have failed to take the message of repentance seriously, and instructs them to abase themselves with sackcloth, ashes and shaven heads.

16. Your city will be saved 92
(God)
To the Ninevites' great joy, God agrees to save their city.

17. God's avenging prophet 94
(Jonah, Ninevites)
Jonah returns, still breathing fire and brimstone, only to be told that God has forgiven the Ninevites and the city's destruction is cancelled. Jonah, far from pleased, stalks away to sit outside the city.

18. The cool ivy tree 97
(Ivy Trees, Solo Worm, Worms)
God provides an ivy tree for Jonah's shelter. The trees take part in a graceful dance as they shield Jonah with their branches. The worms enter and nibble the foliage, killing the tree. The peevish prophet is not pleased!

19. Jonah, stop that sulking 105
(God)
God enlightens Jonah about the irony of his concern for a short-lived tree when he reproaches God for sparing a whole city.

20. Hey Jonah! 106
(All)
Jonah is acclaimed for his eventual obedience and his successful mission to Nineveh as everybody celebrates.

JONAH!

Text and Lyrics: Denis O'Gorman
Music: Barry Hart

1. JONAH, CAN YOU HEAR ME?

God commands Jonah to visit the wicked city of Nineveh and preach a message of repentance. Jonah makes preparations for the journey.

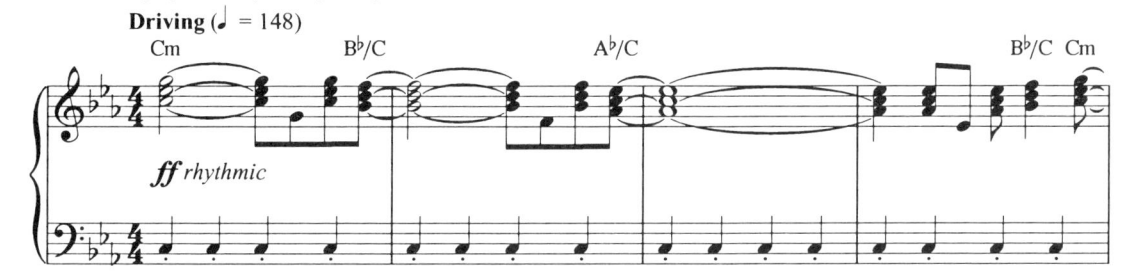

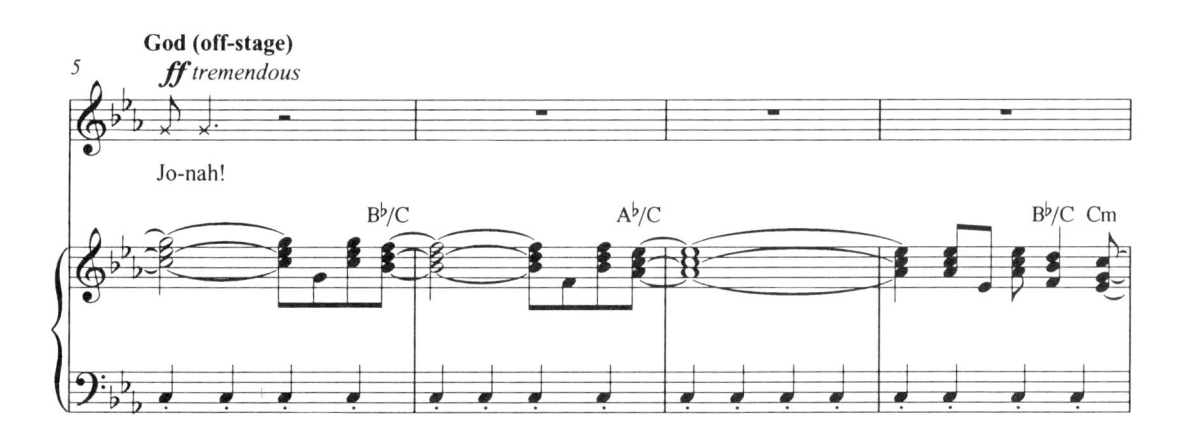

Driving ($\quarternote = 148$)

ff rhythmic

God (off-stage)
ff tremendous

Jo-nah!

Jo-nah!

f spoken (rhythm ad lib.)

Jo-nah, can you
Jo-nah, I'm not

© Copyright 2003 Kevin Mayhew Ltd.
It is illegal to photocopy music.

12

[A♭/C] [Cm]

hear me? Have you got me loud and clear?
fin-ished, I've got some-thing more to say.

15

[B♭/C] [A♭/C] [Cm]

Jo-nah, are you lis-ten-ing? Be-cause I'm look-ing down
Jo-nah, if they keep on sin-ning I swear I'll wipe them all

18

[F/C] [B♭/C] [A♭/C] [Fm/C] [B♭/C] [Cm]

from here. I can see the peo-ple scorn-ing
a-way! Now my an-ger's real-ly blaz-ing!

21

[F/C] [B♭/C] [A♭/C]

ev-'ry sin-gle thing I say. I have caught them do-ing things I could
Jo-nah, you must not de-lay. Hur-ry up for you must preach of my

24   Fm/C   B♭/C   Gsus⁴   G⁷

not men - tion down in the ci - ty of sin that they call
in - ten - tion down in the ci - ty of sin that they call

ff

27   Cm   B♭/D   E♭

Jonah *mf legato, with conviction*

*Ni - ne - veh!   Yes, God, I can
Ni - ne - veh!   Yes, God, I am

mf legato

30   Fm/E♭   E♭maj⁷   E♭6   Fm/E♭   Fm/B♭

hear you speak-ing from the cloud.
with you, just re - ly on me.

33   E♭   Cm   A♭

But, Lord, I im - plore you please don't shout so
Yes, Lord, I'm your ser - vant as I'm sure you

* *Pronounced 'Ninn-uh-vay'*

loud. I a-gree the things that you see must
see. Now I know that I've got to go to

Choir *mf sustained*
Ah,

make you real-ly mad, the deeds they do must
preach in Ni - ne - veh and tell them straight it's

Ah,

an - ger you, I must ad-mit that things are look-ing bad.
not too late, I pro-mise, Lord, I'm leav-ing right a-way.

I must ad-mit that things are look-ing bad.
I pro-mise, Lord, I'm leav-ing right a-way.

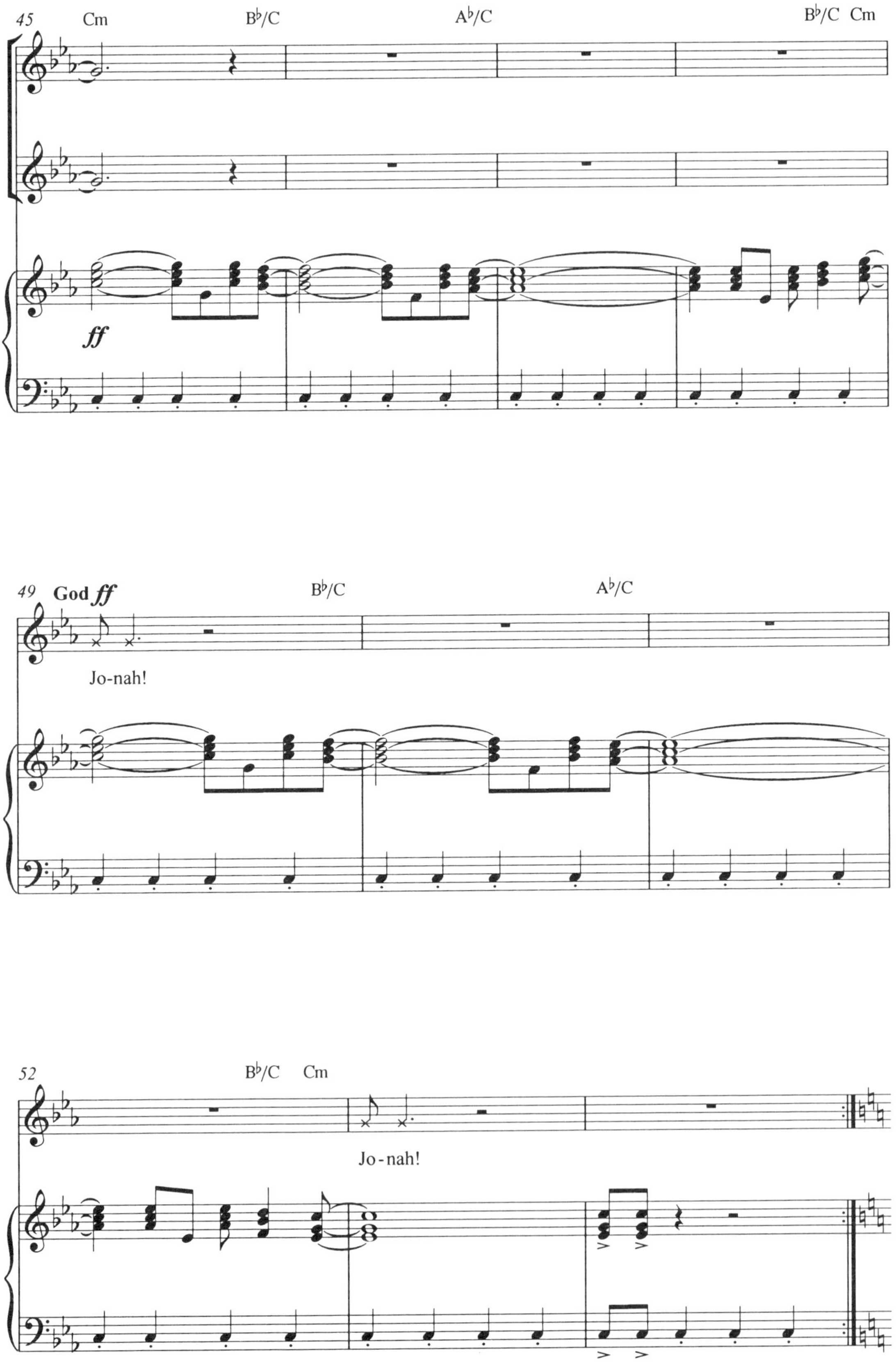
45
Cm
B♭/C
A♭/C
B♭/C Cm
ff
49
God ff
B♭/C
A♭/C
Jo-nah!
52
B♭/C Cm
Jo-nah!

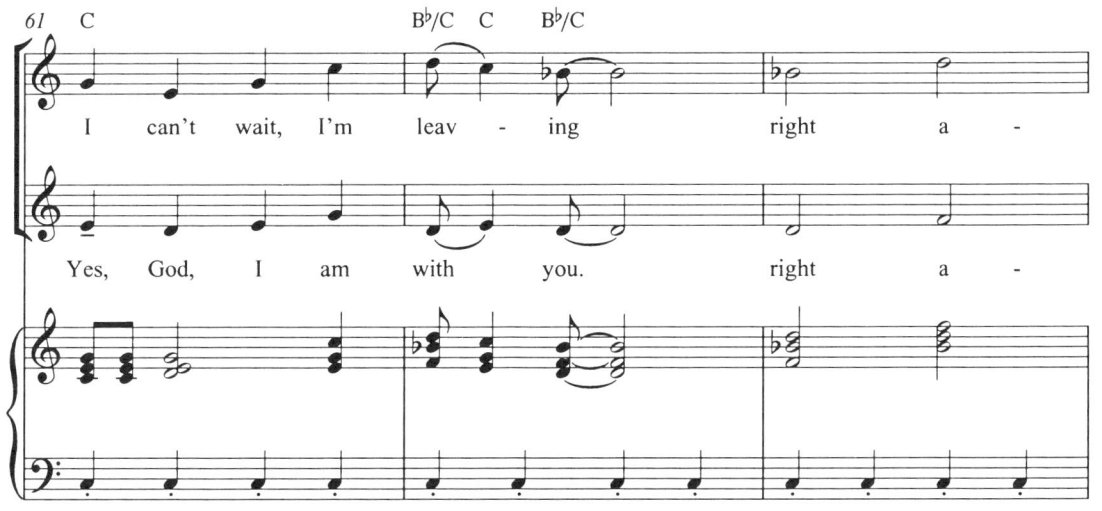

Jonah *f*
I'm not afraid to go there, I'll show them, come what may. I'm gonna be great, Lord, I can't wait, I'm leaving right a-

Choir *f firmly*
Yes, God, I am with you. Yes, God, I am with you. Yes, God, I am with you. right a-

poco cresc.

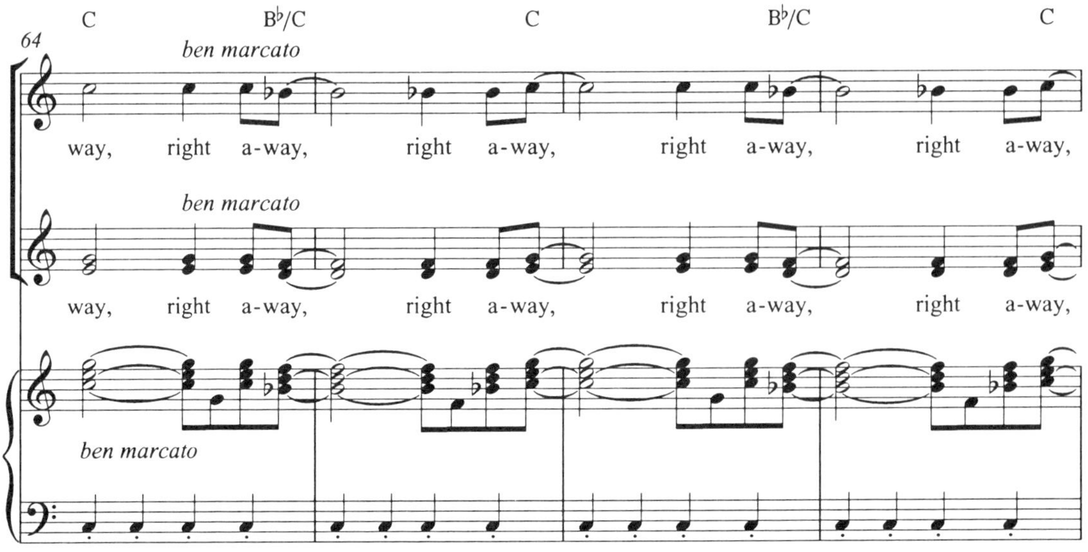
C B♭/C C B♭/C C
64
ben marcato
way, right a-way, right a-way, right a-way, right a-way,
ben marcato
way, right a-way, right a-way, right a-way, right a-way,
ben marcato

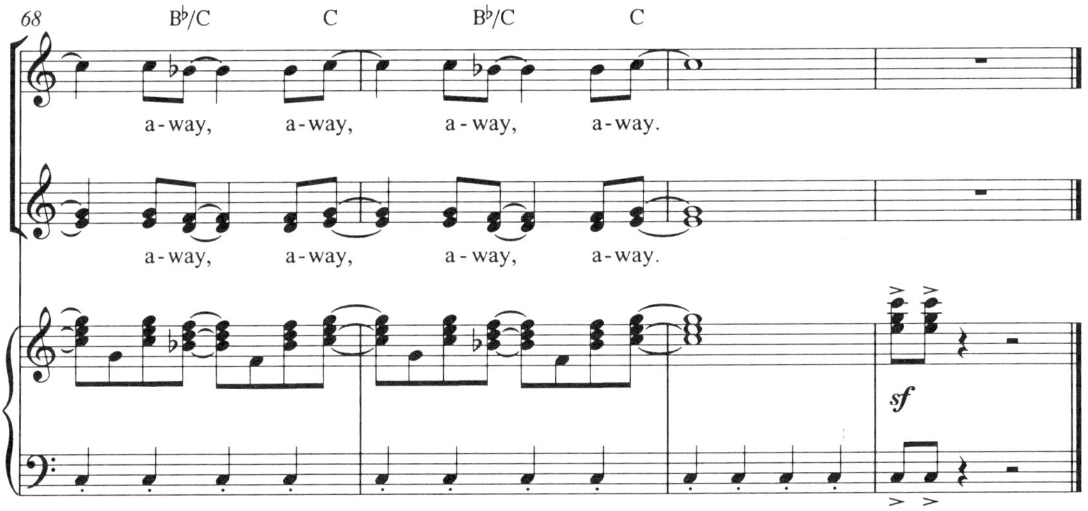
68
B♭/C C B♭/C C
a-way, a-way, a-way, a-way.
a-way, a-way, a-way, a-way.
sf

2. WAIT A MINUTE, JONAH

The Little Devils sow the seeds of doubt in Jonah's mind and tempt him to disobey God's instruction.

Little Devils 1
Wait a minute, Jonah, just before you go, don't you think there's one more thing
Jonah, don't get taken in, what's it got to do with you

Little Devils 2
Wait, wait, wait a minute. Just, just, just before you go. Don't, don't, don't
Think, think, think about it. Don't, don't, don't get taken in. What's, what's, what's

that you ought to know?
if they wan-na sin?

you think? That, that, that you ought to know?
it got? If, if, if they wan-na sin?

13 *marcato*
Ni-ne-veh's a big, bad ci-ty, there's a punch-up e-ve-ry night
Can't you see this deal's one-sid-ed. What your sac-ri-fice will cost?

there's a punch-up e-ve-ry night
What your sac-ri-fice will cost?

marcato

2nd time to Coda
16
and they'll have your guts for gar-ters if you get in a fight.
So get smart, buzz off and scar-per, run a-way and get lost.

your guts for gar-ters if you get in a fight.
buzz off and scar-per, run a-way and get lost.

2nd time to Coda

God will stop at no-thing to get his way.

You're a fool to trust him so get a-way. Don't de-lay. Think a-bout it

You're a fool to trust him so get a-way. Don't de-lay.

Buzz off and scar - per, sling your hook and get lost! Buzz off and scar-per, on your bike and get lost! And get lost!

3. BY JOVE! YOU'RE RIGHT

Jonah runs away from the Lord and decides to catch a ship from Joppa taking him to Tarshish.

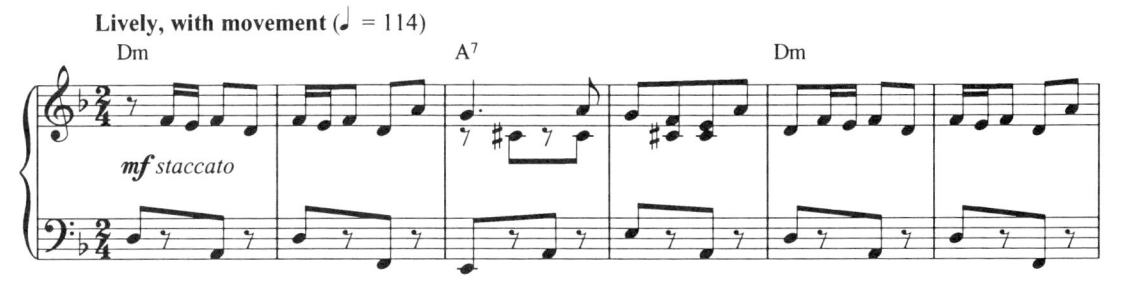

Lively, with movement (♩ = 114)

mf staccato

Jonah *mf precise*
By Jove! You're right, I'm not a Ni-ne-vite. I daren't go there and get in-to a fight. I
just not fair of God to send me there, if I get caught I would-n't have a prayer. I'd

Little Devils / Choir *mf precise*
By Jove! We're right, you're not a Ni-ne-vite. You daren't go there and get in-to a fight.
It's just not fair of God to send you there, if you get caught you would-n't have a prayer.

17

won't o-bey or go to Ni-ne-veh. I'm scared to
soon be dead for they'd cut off my head. If God's so

You won't o-bey or go to Ni-ne-veh. You're scared
You'd soon be dead for they'd cut off your head. If God's

22 **Slower: ad lib.** (♩ = 65)

death, I'd bet-ter run a-way. How I wish my Mom-ma could be here to
brave then he can go in-stead. I am sure that Mom-ma would ap-prove, she

to death, you'd bet-ter run a-way.
so brave then he can go in-stead.

trem.
mp legato

27 **Tempo I**

tell me what to do —
al-ways knows what's best — **Momma** *f raucous*

Jo-nah! Come back home at once, I'm
Jo-nah! I could box your ears, you

Jonah
It's flam-ing mad with you!
So bloomin' lit-tle pest!

Gradually accelerating until the end
So now I'll slip a-way and catch a ship, it's time to go and take a lit-tle trip. I heard them say they

Little Devils / Choir
So now you'll slip a-way and catch a ship, it's time to go and take a lit-tle trip. You heard them say

46
A7 Dm A7
sail from Jop-pa Bay, I must go there and try to get a-
they sail from Jop-pa Bay, you must go there and try to get a-
51
Dm Gm Dm/A Gm6/B♭ Aaug/C♯
way, a-way, a-way, and try to get a-
way, a-way, and try to get a-
f ben marcato
55
Dm N.C. Dm
way! Hey!
way! Hey!
8va

4. JONAH, I CAN SEE YOU

Jonah is on the run, but God keeps a watchful eye on him as he attempts to make good his escape.

Driving (♩ = 148)

ff rhythmic

God *f spoken (rhythm ad lib.)*

Jo-nah, I can see you run-ning but you won't get ve-ry far. Jo-nah, don't you think you've lost me, be-cause I know just where you are.

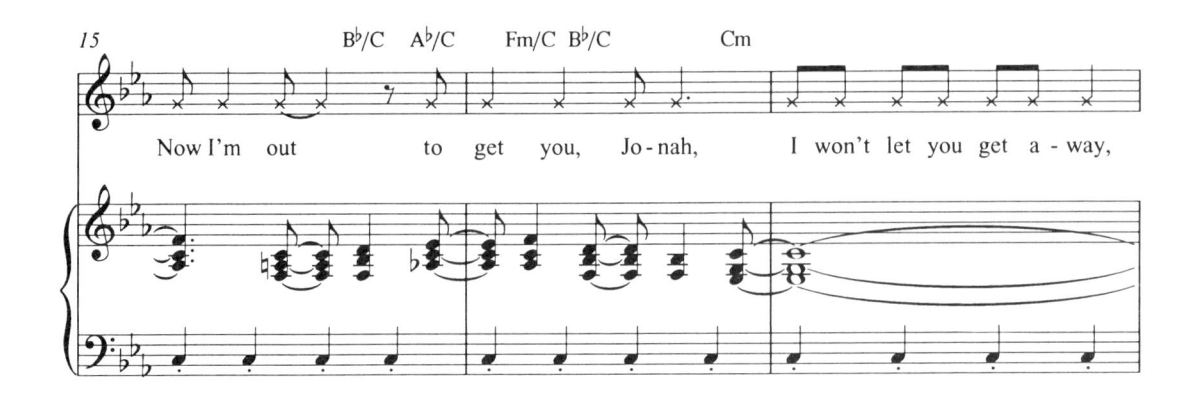

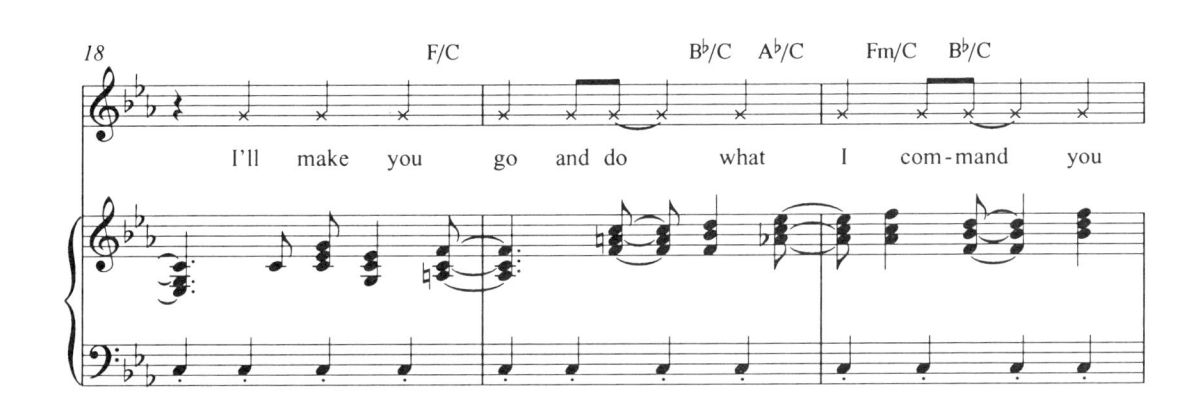

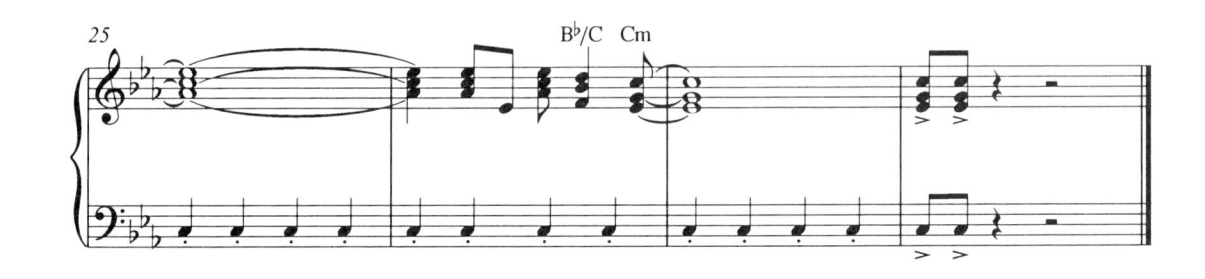

Now I'm out to get you, Jonah, I won't let you get away, I'll make you go and do what I command you down in the city of sin that they call Nineveh!

5. EVERYBODY'S WELCOME TO JOPPA

The port of Joppa is presented as a down-at-heel seaside resort. The holiday-makers, fully kitted out for their annual treat, extol Joppa's many delights; the local children take a more jaundiced view. Jonah, after wandering in and out of the throng, is only too pleased to jump aboard a barely seaworthy vessel and head off to Tarshish as the crowd waves farewell.

Bright and breezy (♩ = 130)

mf rhythmic: staccato feel

Holiday-makers *mf*:
Sun-shine and sand and the Jop-pa Town Band, it's love-ly to be back here once more!
What a great sight, there's pop mu-sic all night that plays non-stop from mid-night till four.

All *f*: Once more! / Till four!

Holiday-makers *mf*:
Down by the sea eat-ing chips on the quay and watch-ing all the boats on the shore.
Ev-'ry-one knows that the pubs ne-ver close, you could-n't ask for a-ny-thing more.

25

Holiday-makers

1. Licking pink candy-floss, sending postcards to the boss, 'Sir, we miss you, wish you were here.' We're having fun getting tanned
2. All the clubs here have blokes telling very funny jokes, 'Nudge, nudge, wink, wink, know what I mean?' Then you can go to a star-

Choir *mf*
La la la la la la la la la la la la la.

16

in the sun and fish - ing off the end of the pier.
- stud - ded show or crown - ing of the car - ni - val queen.

18 **Children/Choir** *mf*

The fun - fair is teem - ing with spot -
You'll find this a - mus - ing, your gran -

Small Group *mf*

The fun - fair is teem - ing with spot -
You'll find this a - mus - ing, your gran -

20 **1: Spotty Kids** *(bawling)*

- ty kids scream - ing, 'I want a big Cheese - bur - ger Whop -
- ny is los - ing at bin - go and no one can stop

- ty kids scream - ing, *(tacet)*
- ny is los - ing at bin - go and no one can stop

Children/Choir

-per!' They're sel-ling choc i - ces at scan-
her. She can't stand the ten - sion, 'I've just

They're sel-ling choc i - ces at scan-
her. She can't stand the ten - sion, *(tacet)*

2: Children/Choir

- da-lous pri - ces, ke-babs on a stick, it's no won-
blown me pen-sion!' But ne-ver you mind, they look out

- da-lous pri - ces, ke-babs on a stick, it's no won-
But ne-ver you mind, they look out

All

-der they're sick, so ev-'ry-bo-dy's wel-come to Jop - pa!
for her kind 'cause ev-'ry-bo-dy's wel-come to Jop-

-der they're sick, so ev-'ry-bo-dy's wel-come to Jop - pa!
for her kind 'cause ev-'ry-bo-dy's wel-come to Jop-

-pa!

Sailors: Who wants a trip on our luxury ship? We're sailing off to Tarshish today. **All:** Today! **Sailors:** Come, ev'ry-one, if you wanna have fun, we're waiting here to take you away. **Captain:** And the ship's in good shape, she's been twice a-round the Cape –

Sailors *mf*
La la la la la

rest as-sured she's safe as can be. If you feel bored we can take

rest as-sured she's safe as a ship can be. If you feel bored we can take

you a-board, we're sail - ing at a quar-ter to three. **All** Hey, you

Small Group
you a-board, we're sail - ing at a quar-ter to three. Hey, you

2: Jonah
3: All   B♭   Cm   **1: Solo** A♭

(1.) must be jok - ing, your fuel tanks are smok - ing, that en -
(2.) take my suit - case, I'm fed up with this place, that sounds
(3.) la la la la la la la la la la la la

must be jok - ing, your fuel tanks are smok - ing. *(tacet)*
(2.) *(tacet)*
(3.) la la la la la la la la la la la la

B♭   E♭   **1, 2, 3: All** E♭/G A♭

- gine will soon come a crop - per!   You'll ne -
like a ve - ry good of - fer.   You must
la la la la la la la.   We can't

                                          You'll ne -
                                          You must
la la la la la la la.   We can't

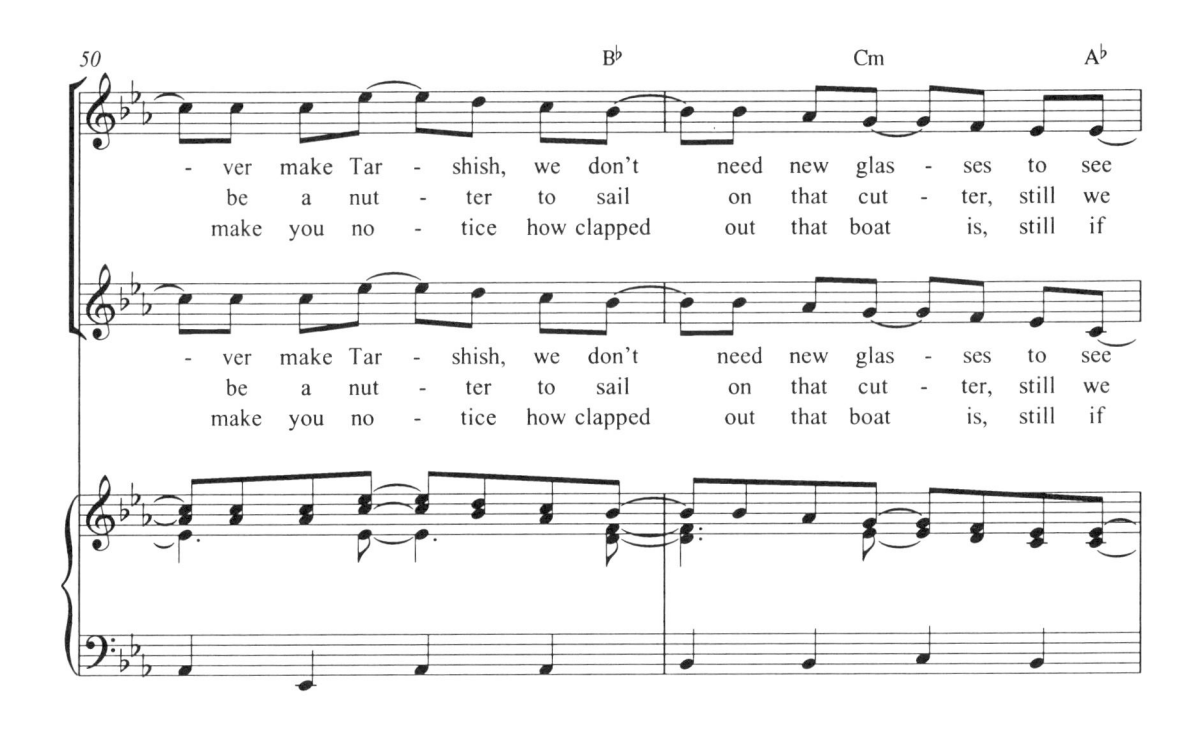

-ver make Tar - shish, we don't need new glas - ses to see
be a nut - ter to sail on that cut - ter, still we
make you no - tice how clapped out that boat is, still if

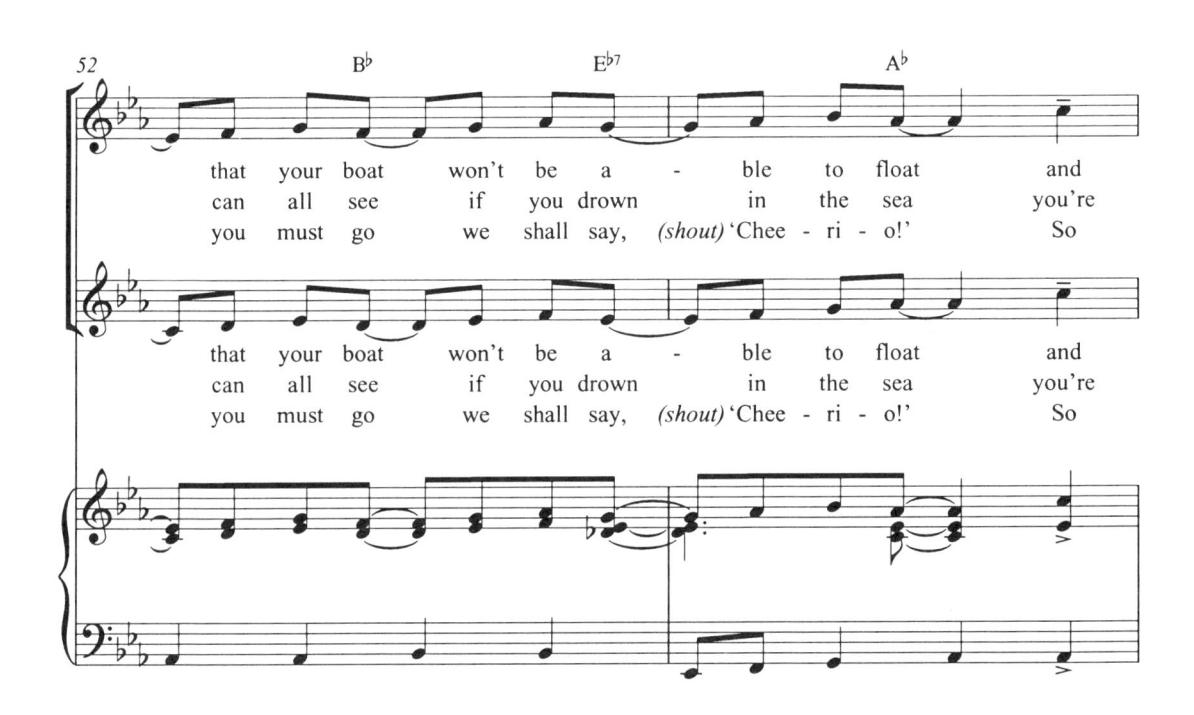

that your boat won't be a - ble to float and
can all see if you drown in the sea you're
you must go we shall say, *(shout)* 'Chee - ri - o!' So

ev-'ry-bo-dy's saf-er in Jop - pa! 2. Hey, here
bet-ter off than liv-ing in Jop - pa! 3. La la

ev-'ry-bo-dy's saf-er in Jop - pa! 2. (tacet)
bet-ter off than liv-ing in Jop - pa! 3. La la

ar - ri - ve - der - ci from, ar - ri - ve - der - ci from,

ar - ri - ve - der - ci from, ar - ri - ve - der - ci from,

ar - ri - ve - der - ci from Jop - pa! Bon voy - age!

ar - ri - ve - der - ci from Jop - pa! Bon voy - age!

6. THE STORM SEQUENCE

The Lord sends a violent storm and the sailors call out to their gods to save them. As they throw the cargo overboard, Jonah is discovered below decks fast asleep. They pick straws to see who is to blame for the storm. Jonah gets the short straw and confesses that it is all his fault for disobeying God. He tells them to throw him overboard and, reluctantly, they agree.

Turbulent ($\quarternote = 160$)
Guitar plays riff based on RH piano part

ff heavily accented

Sailors *f with urgency*

Hear that thun-der, A-shur's an-gry, Ne-gal's hop-pin' mad.
They won't ans-wer, no-thing's hap-pened, they don't wan-na know!

2nd time: Captain

Ish-tar's fum-ing, A-dad's rag-ing;
Chuck the car-go, drop the an-chor,

34

things are look-ing bad. / *clear the decks be-low.*

Sailors *sustained for 3 bars*

Migh-ty gods, we've got the mes-sage, can't you tone it down? We beg you Sham-mash, Ne-go, Nush-ka, Mar-duk, please we don't wan-na drown!

O-kay, Cap-tain, let's get mov-ing, leave the gods a-lone. It's clear that we must ride this storm with-out them 'cause now we're on our own!

ff *shouted*

Guitar riff as previously

27
2.
Solo 1 mf
The
2.
Guitar riff as previously
mf
29
Am
gods are an-gry and some-one round here's to blame.
picked a long straw, no - bo - dy can blame me.
32
2: Solo 3
We bet-ter pick straws 'cause we got - ta find out his
And mine is the same, take a look for your - self and
35
Dm Dm7 Dm
Sailors f
name.
see.
Hey you! What
O - kay, stran -
f

38
Am Dm Dm7 Dm Am
you do - ing, stran - ger? Wake up! We are all in dan - ger,
- ger, now it's your go. Come on, o - pen up your hand so
1.
41 Fmaj7 Fmaj7/6 E7 N.C. Am
so you bet - ter join in too – 'cause it might be you.
1.
2.
44
Solo 2
Fmaj7 E7 Eaug E7
ben marcato
I've ev - 'ry - one can see if it is ...
2.
ben marcato

Moving along - gospel style

Solo 1:
Wow! It's you, you're the one to blame! You might as well con-fess. It's not our gods, it's yours, you know, who went and got us in this mess!
Your God sure is mad with you and got you on the run, so spill the beans, start talk-ing now and tell us what it is you've done!

Sailors:
It's you, you're the one to blame! You might as well con-fess. Oo doop doop b' doop doop doop doop doop doop who went and got us in this mess, this mess!
Your God sure is mad with you and got you on the run, and tell us what it is you've done!

56
D A/E C#7/E# F#m E D A
Tell us, now tell us, why did you have to
Tell us, now tell us, why did you have to
59
B7 E7 A A7
leave home and run? You've been up to some - thing 'cause he
leave home and run? Doop doop b' doop doop doop
61
D F#dim A/E B7/F# E7 F#m
did-n't do this for no - thing so tell us what it is you've done,
dop doop doop so tell us what it is you've done,

63
just you tell us what it is you've

just you tell us what it is you've

A little slower (♩ = 154)

66 Jonah *mf fervently, very sustained*
I am a He-brew Jo-nah, I should be in Ni-ne-veh.

Sailors
done!

mf legato

70
In a dream I heard God cal-ling, 'Jo - nah, do not de-lay.'

Choir *mf*
'Jo - nah, do not de-lay.'

74
F♯m
Bm7
E
F♯m
I knew I could-n't face them, so I dis - o - beyed the Lord.
I knew I could-n't face them, so I dis - o - beyed the Lord.
78
D
A/E
E/G♯
Dmaj7
E
F♯m
E
f
If you want to calm this tem-pest, throw me in the sea and leave me.
If you want to calm this tem-pest, throw me in the sea and leave me.
82
Dmaj7
E
F♯m
E/D
A/G♯
C♯m/E
ff
Throw me, it's the truth, be - lieve me. Throw me
Throw me, it's the truth, be - lieve me. Throw me

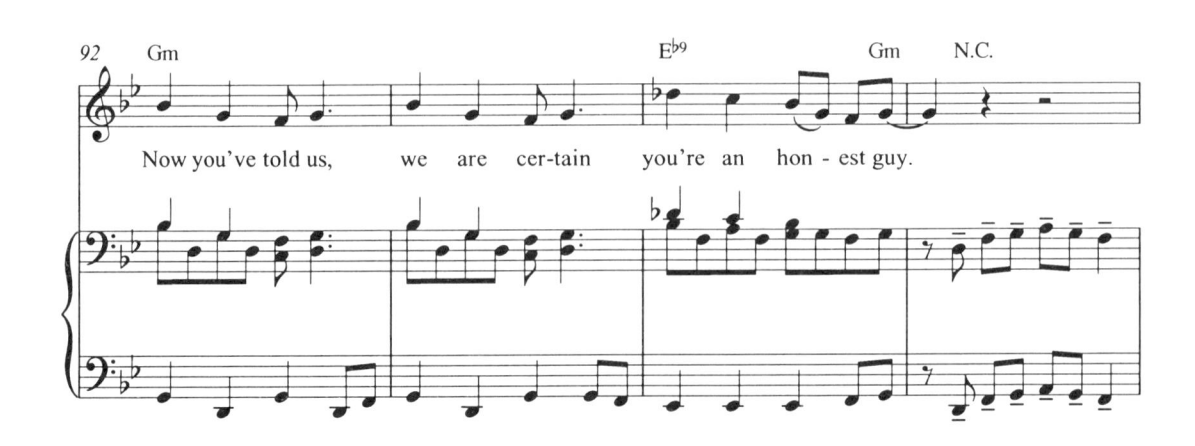

Sailors

Cool it, Jo-nah, we won't harm you, we won't let you die.

Now you've told us, we are cer-tain you're an hon-est guy.

E♭ N.C. F Gm N.C. F/A B♭ N.C. Cm/E♭ F D D7
96 Sailors 1
May - be God will let us row a - no - ther mile or two. We beg you
Sailors 2 f
May - be God will let us row a mile or two. We beg you
100 Gm E♭9
God, you saved the ark of No - ah, Lord
God, you saved the ark of No - ah, Lord
D7 N.C. Gm E♭ F
103 Jonah ff
come and save us too. No! Throw me in the sea!
ff
come and save us too. Row!
ff

No! Can't I make you see? No! I've be-trayed the
Row!
Lord! No! Throw me o-ver-board! Then
Row!
go go go go go go go go GO!

7. BYE, BYE, JONAH

The storm quietens and, standing on the side of the ship, the sailors sing a tearful farewell.

Quasi-barbershop style (♩ = 72)

Solo Sailor: *mp plaintively, slightly tongue-in-cheek*

So it's bye, bye, Jo-nah, bye, bye, Oo, (Oo).

Sailors: Oo, (Oo).

What a sport-ing fel-low, a real-ly good guy. We're so

We're so

45

9
G B7 Baug B7 Em Cm6/A Cm
mf intensely
sad you have to leave us, it's true, please be - lieve us,
mf intensely
sad you have to leave us, it's true, please be - lieve us,
mf
13
G/D Dm6/B E E7 Am6/F♯ E7/G♯ Am7 Em/B
mp
we could sit down and cry – so now it's bye, bye,
mp
boo boo hoo boo hoo, so now it's bye, bye,
mp
18
C C9 N.C. Cm G6
rall.
Jo - nah, Jo - nah, bye, bye, bye. (tears)
Jo - nah,
rall.

8. UNDERWATER DANCE SEQUENCE

The sea creatures join in a movement sequence. The dance builds to a climax and they scatter as God calls Jonah again. They 'swim' to the side of the stage revealing Jonah's inert body lying on the sea bed.

Flowing: tempo rubato ($\quarternote = 74$)

Shoals of fishes

mp very sustained

Brisk military tempo ($\quarternote = 108$)
Sea Horses

rall.

f *sprightly, staccato style*

mp

Light and jazzy
Crabs

49

All the Sea Creatures

f more vigorously

God *(shouted)* Jo - nah!

ff

Attacca

9. JONAH, LOOK AROUND YOU

God sends a whale to swallow Jonah. Where elaborate staging is not possible, complete darkness with Jonah in a single spot should suggest his incarceration.

Driving (♩ = 148) — *sea creatures scatter, revealing Jonah's inert body. Slowly he revives.*

ff rhythmic

God (off-stage) *ff tremendous*

Jo-nah! Jo-nah! Jo-nah! look a-round you, I hope you're wet and cold.

Now I'm going to teach you to do what you've been told! Though I've calmed the sea above you, believe me I'm not through, I'm sending a gigantic whale and, Jonah, I will make it swallow you!

The whale approaches

The whale swallows Jonah

Sombre: moderate two in a bar ($\boldsymbol{\mathit{d}} = 74$)

God Jo-nah, just you stay there for now you're in dis-grace. You'll find it most un-pleas-ant in that dark and smel-ly place. May-be that will teach you that I al-ways get my way. I've locked you up in-side a whale and that's where you will stay.

rall.

Attacca

10. YAHWEH, PLEASE DON'T LEAVE ME

Jonah repents, and as the music broadens in the final verse, he begins to see the light and is eventually vomited onto dry land.

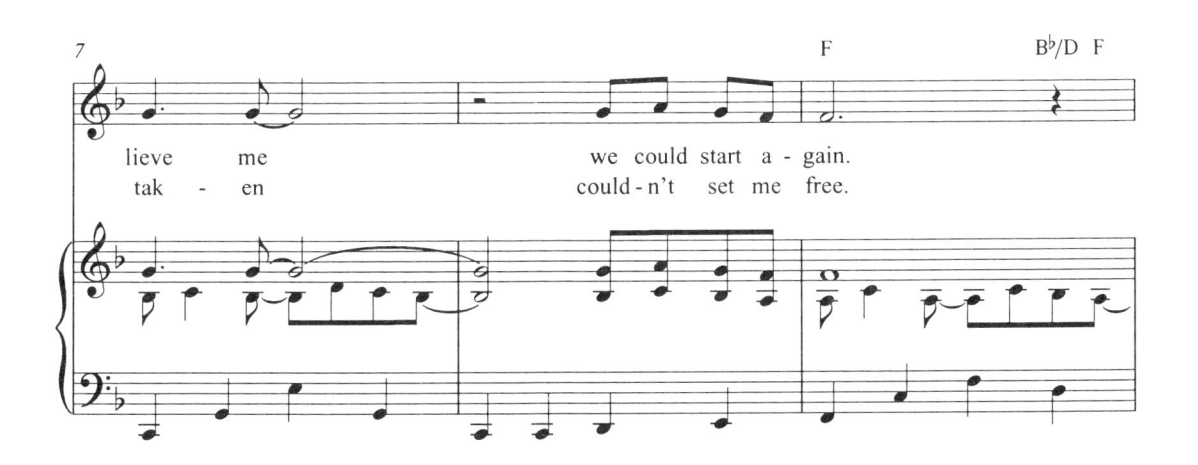

Beseeching (♩ = 88)

Jonah mp

1st time Guitar tacet

Yah-weh, please don't leave me,
sa - ken,
bro-ken and in pain;
now at last I see
Fa-ther, please be-
that the path I've
lieve me
tak - en
we could start a-gain.
could-n't set me free.

55

10

Gm F/A   F7

Master, can you hear me? Are you still out
Lord, I dis-o-beyed you, thought I'd be all

13 B♭2   Csus4   C7   Dm   *cresc.*

there?   Tell me you're still near me in this
right;   now God, please show mer - cy on your

16 B♭   F/A   **1.** C   *mp*
    mf

hour of my dark   des - pair.   Lone-ly and for-
ser-vant down here to -

2. Più mosso
Tenderly (♩ = 94)
C Fm B♭m2 B♭m
Sea Creatures mp sustained
night. Jo - nah, have no fear,
Choir mp sustained
Jo - nah, have no fear,
mp sempre legato
Fm Fm/E♭ D♭7 C7 Fm
cresc.
though you have fal - len far down here. Jo - nah,
B♭m2 B♭m E♭7 D♭/A♭ A♭maj7
mf
don't des-pair, sure - ly the Lord has heard your prayer,

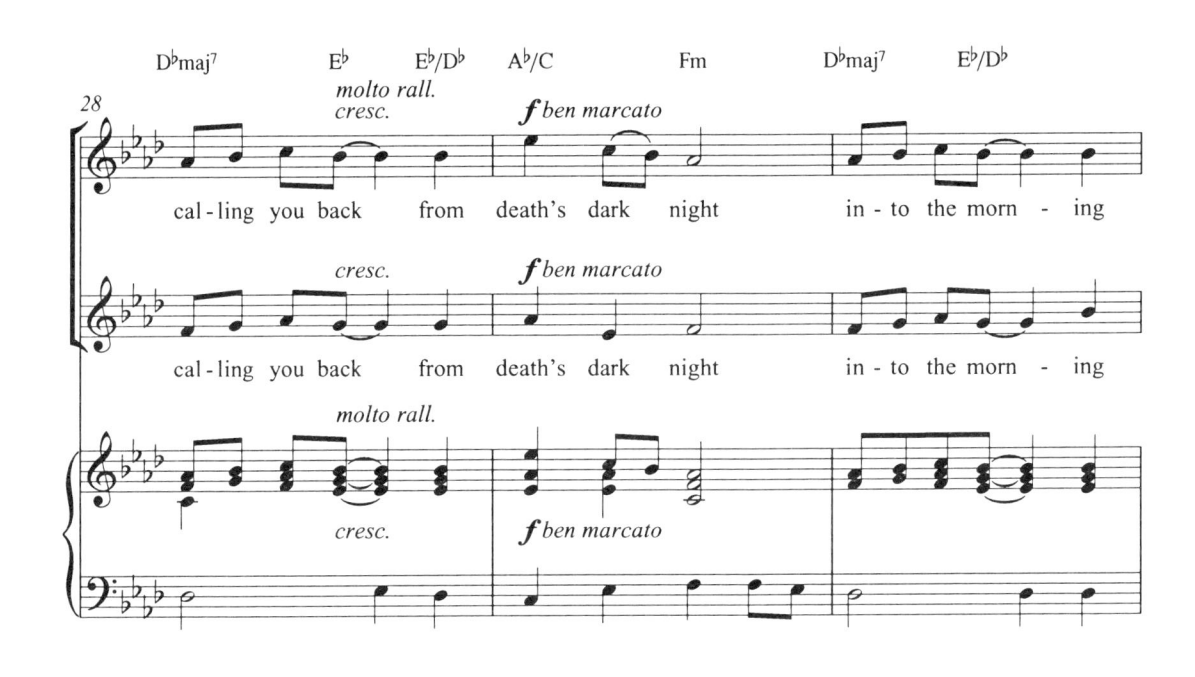

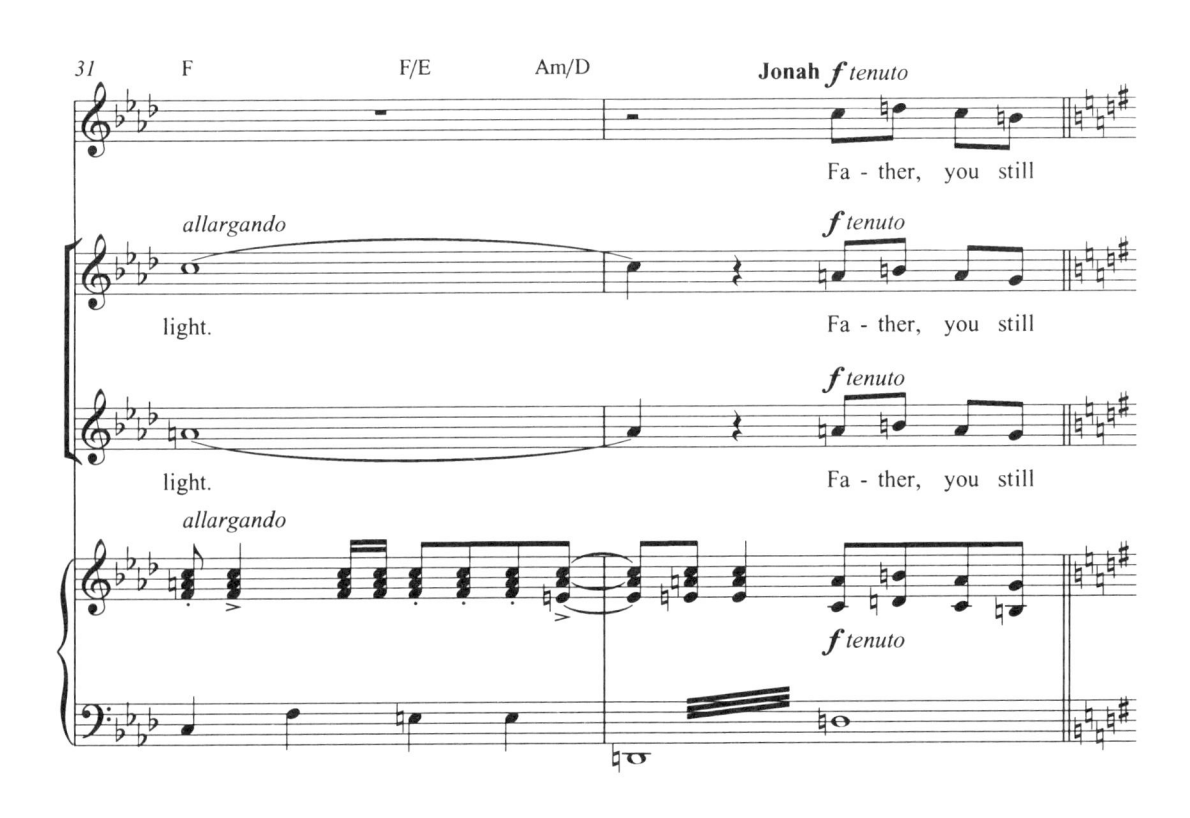

[m. 28] D♭maj7 | E♭ E♭/D♭ | A♭/C Fm | D♭maj7 E♭/D♭

molto rall.
cresc. ***f*** *ben marcato*

cal-ling you back from death's dark night in-to the morn - ing

cresc. ***f*** *ben marcato*

cal-ling you back from death's dark night in-to the morn - ing

molto rall.
cresc. ***f*** *ben marcato*

[m. 31] F | F/E Am/D | **Jonah** ***f*** *tenuto*

allargando ***f*** *tenuto*

light. Fa - ther, you still

light. Fa - ther, you still

allargando ***f*** *tenuto*

f *tenuto*

Very broad - strict tempo again

33 G   C/E   G   D⁷

Jonah
love me, I can see the light

Choir
love me, I can see the light

36
shi-ning up a-bove me, ev-'ry-thing's all

shi-ning up a-bove me, ev-'ry-thing's all

39 G   C/E   G   Am   G/B

right. I can feel the sun-shine,

right. I can feel the sun-shine,

I can see the sky, I know it's a sure sign that you won't leave me here to die.

I shall rise again. I shall rise a-

Yes, God, I am with you,

61

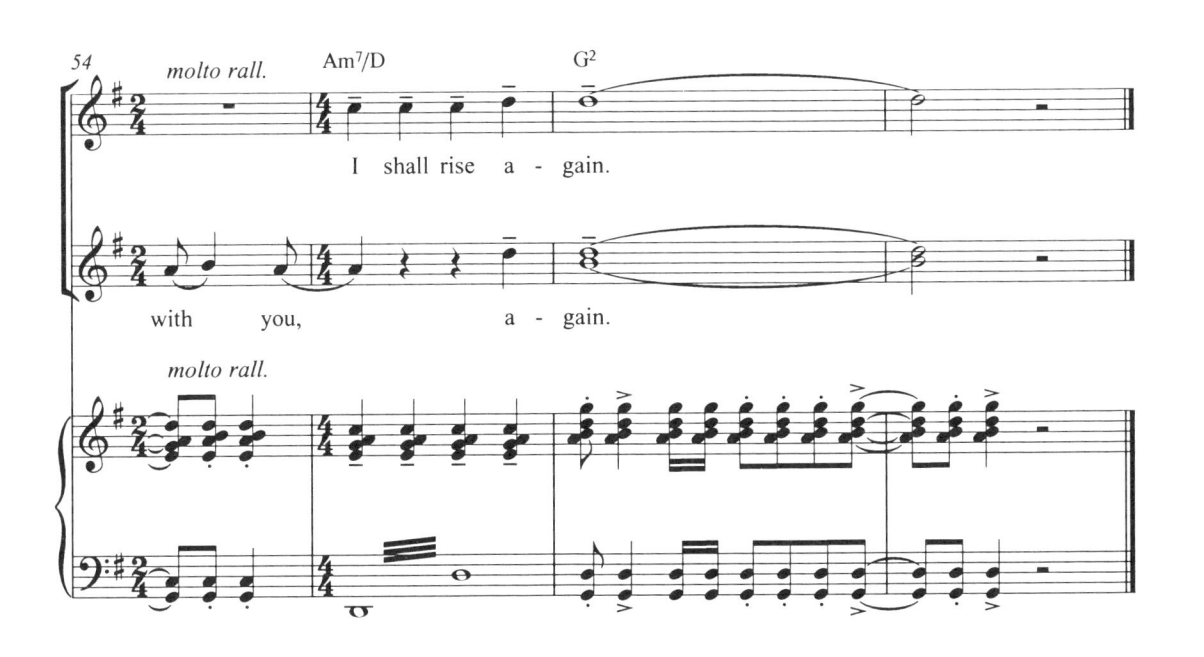

11. SIN CITY

Jonah arrives at Nineveh to find a spectacular rock 'n' roll sequence in full swing.

Lively rock 'n' roll tempo ($\quarternote = 144$)

f marcato

Ninevites and Choir
mf

Rock - in' round the streets of Sin Ci - ty,
Rock - in' round the streets of Sin Ci - ty,

ba - by, bet - ter hold on tight.
we'll go bop - pin' all night long.

Come on, let your hair down, see what's cook - in' down town, we
All the ci - ty's rav - in', hap - py mis - be - ha - vin', groov -

11

could have a ball to-night. So let's sing
-in' as we're mov-in' a - long. Ev-'ry-one

13

as we swing to the beat of the mu-sic,
hav-in' fun giv-in' wild, cra-zy par-ties,

15

shak-in' as we twist and jive.
this could real-ly blow your mind.

17

Stay be-side me, ho-ney, watch me spend m' mo-ney,
Ba-by, don't you leave me, su - gar, please be-lieve me,

Ni - ne - veh is com - in' a - live! Yeah!
ev - 'ry - thin' is gon - na be fine! Yeah!

Ninevites and Choir
Rock - in', rol - lin', ba - by, can't you see you

Little Devils
Rock - in', rol - lin', ba - by, can't you see you

could have a good time, rock - in' round with me?

could have a good time, rock - in' round with me?

25 F⁷   Caug/F   F⁷

Ho - ney, won't you put your hand in mine?

Ho - ney, won't you put your hand in mine?

27 B♭   E♭   B♭   B♭⁷

You send shi - vers down my spine!

You send shi - vers down my spine!

29 E♭   B♭

When I'm with you ev - 'ry - thin's all right, babe,

When I'm with you ev - 'ry - thin's all right, babe,

31

you drive me cra - zy when you hold me tight.

you drive me cra - zy when you hold me tight.

33 F⁷   Bdim   C⁷

A - ny - thing you want now, just let me know,

A - ny - thing you want now, just let me know, know, know,

35   F⁷   B♭

come on and let your - self go!

let your - self go!

67

43
F7
B♭
Oo doo wop b' doo di doo,
Oo doo wop b' doo di doo,
45
Oo doo wop b' doo di doo,
Oo doo wop b' doo di doo,
47
B♭7
E♭
Oo doo wop b' doo di doo,
Oo doo wop b' doo di doo,

49
F7
Gb7
mp cresc. molto
aah, aah,
mp cresc. molto
aah, aah,
mp cresc. molto
51
G7
C7 N.C. C7 N.C.
ff
aah, yeah!
ff
aah, yeah!
ff ben marcato
sf
53
F
C
f
Rock - in', rol - lin', ba - by, can't you see you
f
Rock - in', rol - lin', ba - by, can't you see you
f

55
could have a good time, rock - in' round with me?
could have a good time, rock - in' round with me?
57
G7
Daug/G
G7
Ho - ney, won't you put your hand in mine?
Ho - ney, won't you put your hand in mine?
59
C
F
C
C7
You send shi - vers down my spine!
You send shi - vers down my spine!

61 F — C

When I'm with you ev-'ry-thin's all right, babe,

When I'm with you ev-'ry-thin's all right, babe,

63

you drive me cra-zy when you hold me tight.

you drive me cra-zy when you hold me tight.

65 G⁷ — C♯aug — D⁷

A-ny-thing you want now, just let me know,

A-ny-thing you want now, just let me know, know, know,

71

67
G7
C
come on and let your - self go!
let your - self go!
69
G7
C♯aug
D7
A - ny-thing you want now, just let me know.
A - ny-thing you want now, just let me know, know, know.
71
D7
F♯6
G7
D7
F♯6
G7
Come on! And let! Come on! And let!
Come on! And let! Come on!

74
D7
F#6
G7
N.C.
Come on and let your - self
And let! And let! Come on and let your - self
77
C
C/E
F7
F#dim
go! Go! Go! Go!
go! Go! Go! Go!
79
N.C.
C
Come on, pret - ty ba - by, won't y' let your - self go! Yeah!
Come on, pret - ty ba - by, won't y' let your - self go! Yeah!
sf

12. REPENT!

Dramatically, Jonah declares his message of repentance - or else!

Vigorously (♩ = 160)

ff very rhythmic

Powerfully

do-la-tors! Re-pent! You sin-ful, wick-ed men. You've of-fend-ed Yah-weh but you won't do that a-gain. You'll be shak-ing like a leaf when you hear what's in store. For *hea-then, pa-gan scum like you will burn! burn! burn! for e-ver-more!*

13. BYE, BYE, JONAH

The far from contrite Ninevites take Jonah prisoner and plan a little supper for the gods!

Threatening ($\h = 80$)
High Priest *(rhythm ad lib.)*

mp darkly melodramatic voice

Oo, just look, what have we here? What a funny little chap! So bold, so brave and so sincere, you've fallen in our lap.

accel. e cresc. poco a poco
increasingly menacing

You came here to cause a fuss, to preach on sin and vice. In-

accel. poco a poco
cresc. poco a poco

Faster ($\h = 108$)
f elated: high-pitched voice

stead you've come and given us — a perfect sacrifice!

Lively swing tempo (in 2) ($\halfnote = 108$)

Ninevites and Choir

light and rhythmic, staccato feel

Migh-ty Ne-gal, here's your din-ner, how d'you want him done?
like him cut in sli-ces, boiled with cook-in sauce?

As a spi-cy bur-ger in a dou-ble-deck-er bun?
Tart-ed up with lots of spi-ces for your se-cond course?

Would you like him toast-ed, roast-ed, quite well done or rare? We could
Take your time, you need-n't hur-ry, we could mince and stir what's left

stew him, bar-be-cue him, a-ny-time or a-ny-where. Or would you
o-ver in a cur-ry, simp-ly say what you pre-

fer. So it's bye, bye, Jo-nah, bye, bye, Oo.

Handmaidens *mf*
bye, bye, Jo-nah, bye, bye, Oo.

Ne-gal wants his din-ner, so now you must die.

Ne-gal din-ner, now you must die.

'Cause when stran-gers come to meet 'im, he

stran-gers come to meet 'im, he

just wants to eat 'em, boiled or baked in a pie-

so now it's bye, bye, Jo-nah,

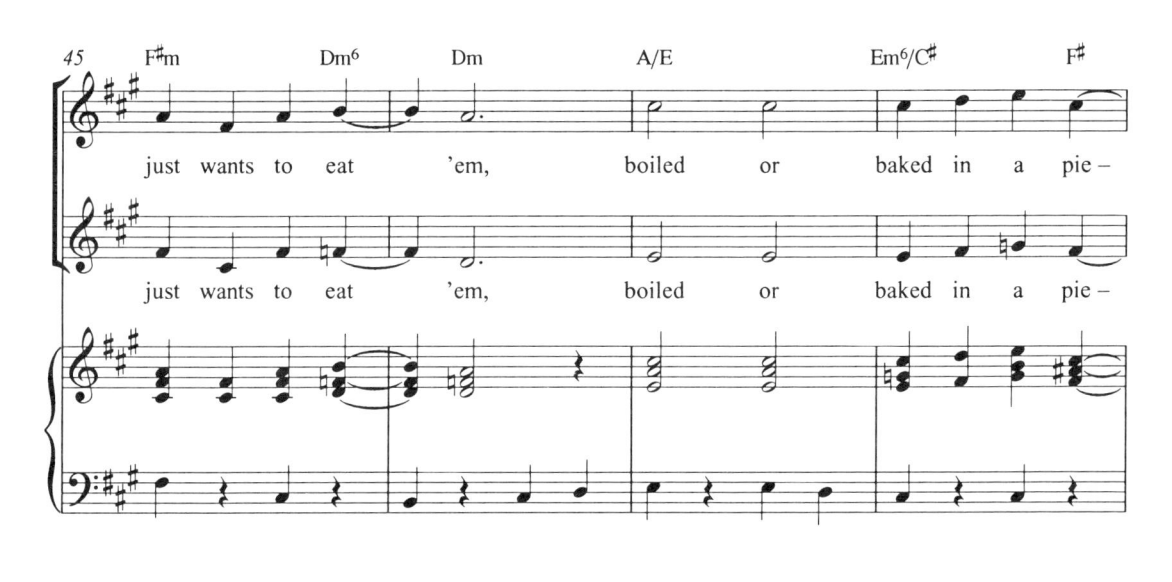

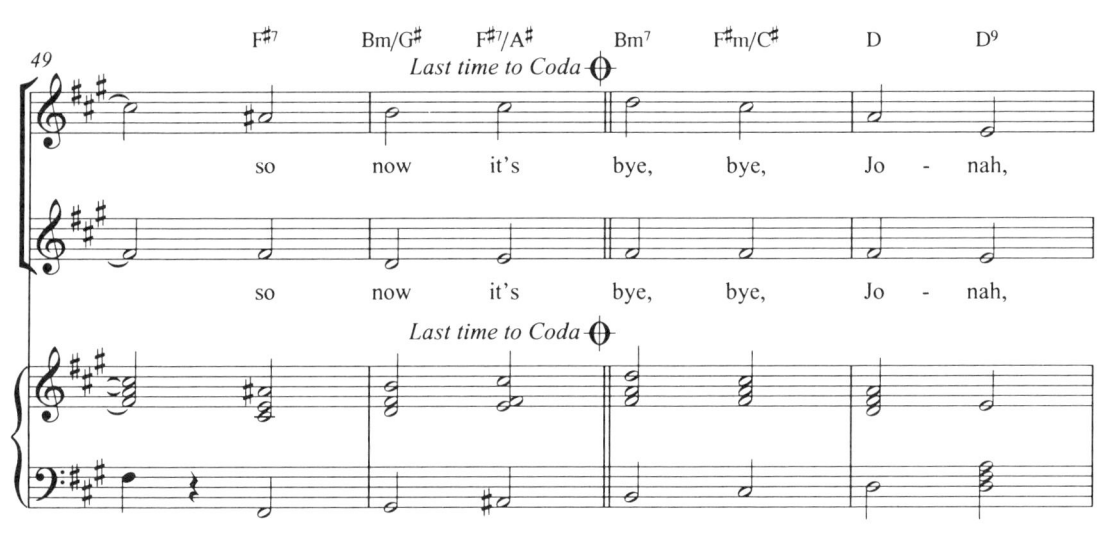

Last time to Coda

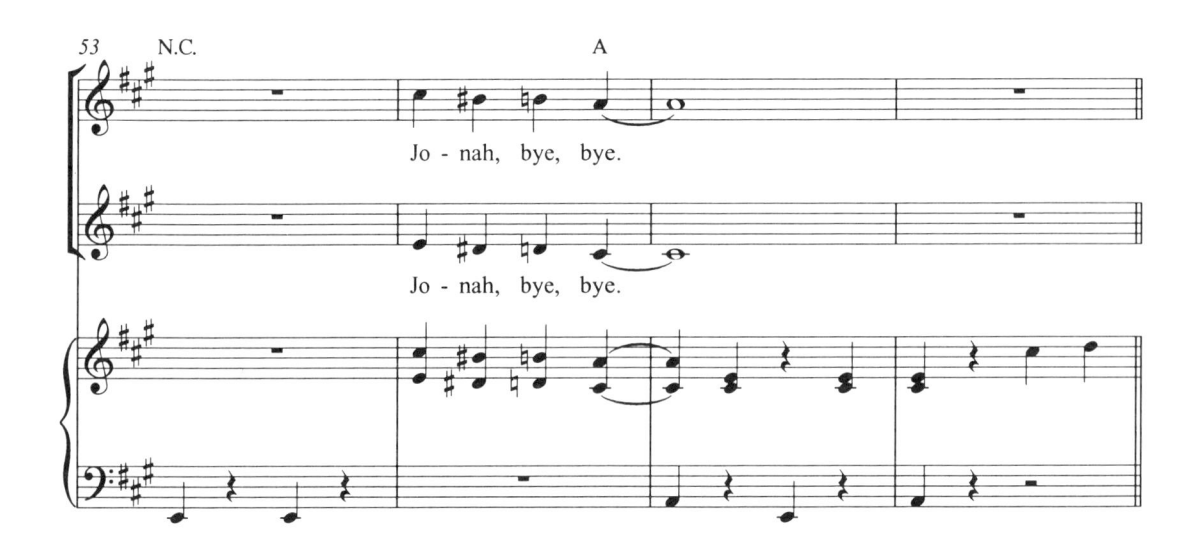

Jo-nah, bye, bye.

Ninevites and Handmaidens
staccato - precise

Doo doo doo doo doo doo doo doo.

High Priest

Ne-gal's get-ting thin-ner so he needs a big-ger din-ner like you.
Ne-gal's tum is rum-bling so we got-ta stop him grum-bling right now.

Doo doo doo doo doo doo doo doo.

Ne-gal says he's starv-ing so we bet-ter start with carv-ing up you.
Now we got the ven-ue we must work out Ne-gal's me-nu some-how.

doo doo doo doo doo doo.

We must
He could

do what Ne - gal wish - es, serve you up on sil - ver dish - es and you'll
have your nose for start - ers, eat your toes with fried to - ma - ters, then your

real - ly taste de - li - cious in a stew!
legs with chi - po - la - tas right

Ninevites

So it's

now!

CODA
Bm7 F#m/C# D D9 Bm7 F#m/C# D D9
74
Ninevites
f
bye, bye, Jo - nah, bye, bye, Jo - nah,
Handmaidens
f
bye, bye, Jo - nah, bye, bye, Jo - nah,
CODA
78
Bm7 F#m/C# D D9 N.C.
bye, bye, Jo - nah, Jo - nah, bye, bye,
bye, bye, Jo - nah, Jo - nah, bye, bye,
82
A
Jo - nah, bye, bye, Jo - nah, bye, bye, ciao!
Jo - nah, bye, bye, Jo - nah, bye, bye, ciao!
sf

14. GOD'S AVENGING PROPHET

Breaking free, Jonah repeats his warning and exits.

Powerfully (♩ = 160)

f very rhythmic

Jonah: Don't you touch me! One more step and you'll go up in flames! I am God's a-veng-ing pro-phet sent to take your names. One by one he'll pun-ish you and no one can re-sist. Just one step, I'm

14   B♭   C   D

warn-ing you, and you'll be on my list!

18 Dm   Am⁷

Start re-pent-ing, on your knees, you'd bet-ter hear me through.

21   Dm

Af-ter watch-ing all your sin-ning,

24 Am⁷   B♭/D

***p** cresc. poco a poco*

God is mad with you. Change your ways or

***p** cresc. poco a poco*

he will send a plague up-on your town, then re-turn in for-ty days and burn, burn, burn, your ci-ty down!

15. SHOW HIM YOU'RE REPENTING

The king is appalled that his subjects have failed to take the message of repentance seriously, and instructs them to abase themselves with sackcloth, ashes and shaven heads.

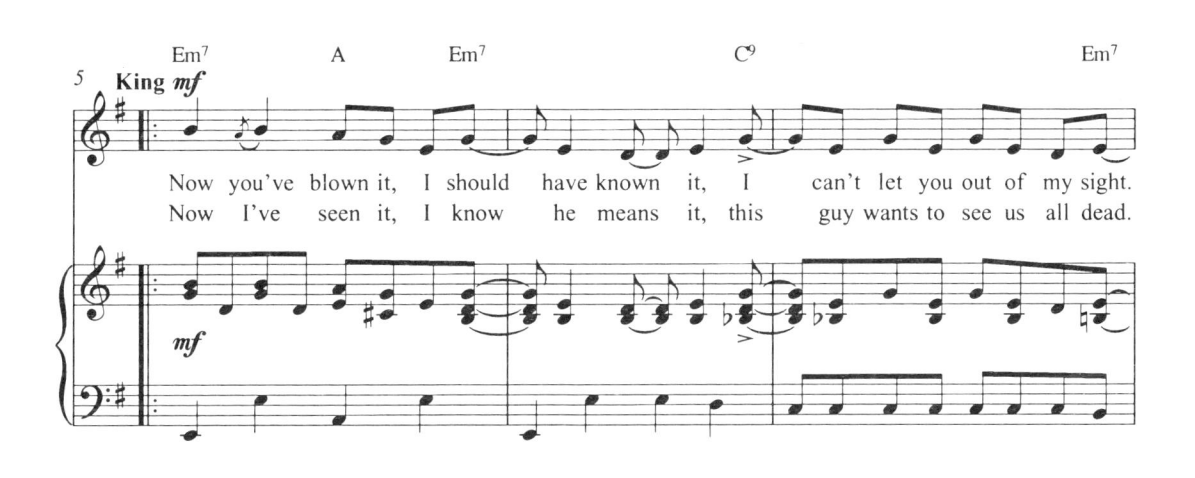

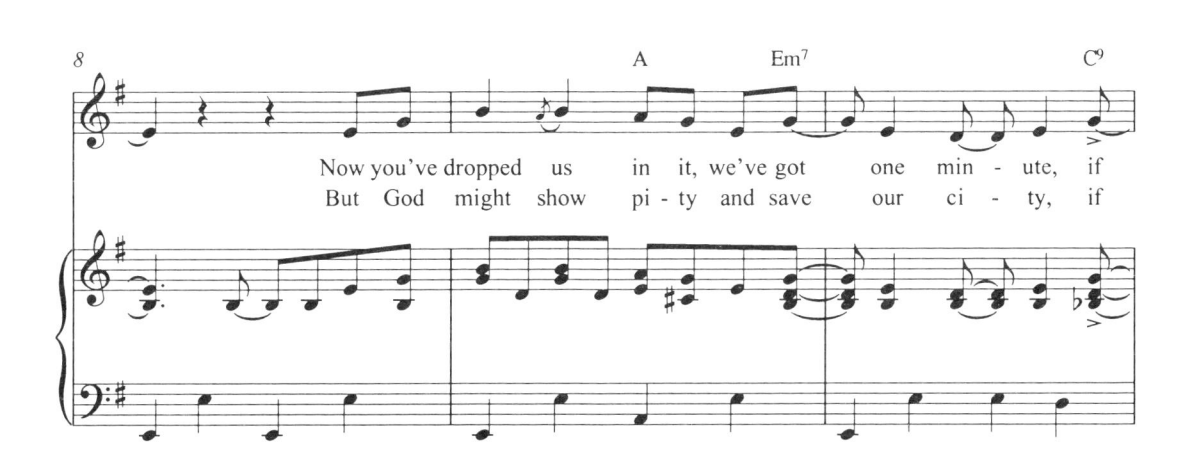

Moving along ($\sqrt{}$ = 156)

f ben marcato

King *mf*

Now you've blown it, I should have known it, I can't let you out of my sight.
Now I've seen it, I know he means it, this guy wants to see us all dead.

Now you've dropped us in it, we've got one min-ute, if
But God might show pi-ty and save our ci-ty, if

we're gon-na put things right. Grab some hair-shirts, start re-pent-
we do the things he said. Call on Yah-weh, kneel be-fore

Ninevites and Choir *mf*
Aah,

-ing! Put on ash-es, start la-ment-ing! Get that
him. Raise your hands high and a-dore him, show this

aah, aah, aah. Get that
show this

ben marcato
hair cut off your head; show him you're re-
pro-phet you have changed; show him you're re-

ben marcato
hair cut off your head;
pro-phet you have changed;

ben marcato

20 Em7
Asus4 A7
pent - ing.
Show him you're re -
pent - ing.
Show him you're re -
We're sor - ry, did - n't mean to do it!
22 Em7
Asus4 A7
pent - ing.
pent - ing.
We're sor - ry, did - n't mean to do it!
24 Em7 A7sus4 A7 Em7 N.C.
f
27 Em7 Em7 A7sus4 A7 Em7

30 N.C. Em7 King mf B6 B B7 Esus4
Call on Yah - weh, kneel be - fore
Ninevites and Choir mf
Aah,
mf
33 Em D6 D D7 Gsus4 G f
him. Raise your hands high and a - dore him, show this
aah, aah, aah, show this
f
36 Am Am7 Am6 Am7 B7 N.C.
ben marcato
pro - phet you have changed; show him you're re -
ben marcato
pro - phet you have changed;
ben marcato

39 *Em⁷* ... *Asus⁴* *A⁷*

pent - ing. Show him you're re -
We're sor - ry, did - n't mean to do it!

41 *Em⁷* ... *Asus⁴* *A⁷*

pent - ing. Show him you're re -
We're sor - ry, did - n't mean to do it!

43 *Em⁷* *Asus⁴* *A⁷* *Em⁷* Guitar plays melody

ff

pent - ing. Show him you're re - pent - ing. Show him you're re - pent - ing!
Show him you're re - pent - ing. Show him you're re - pent - ing!

16. YOUR CITY WILL BE SAVED

To the Ninevites' great joy, God agrees to spare their city.

Driving ($\quarternote = 148$)

ff rhythmic

God *(conciliatory but still firm)* **mf** *spoken (rhythm ad lib.)*

All right now, that's e-nough, I can see your heads are shaved. You're look-ing quite re-pen-tant so your ci-ty will be saved. *loud cheer from the Ninevites*

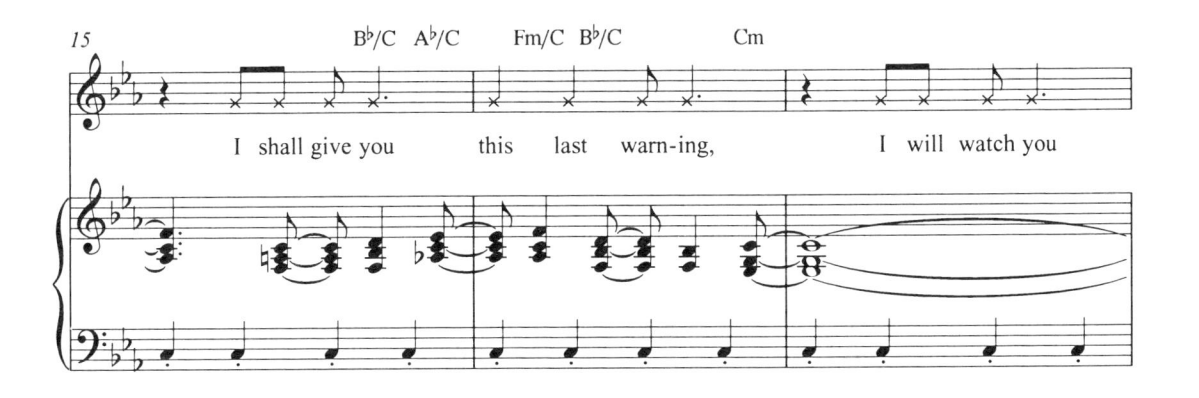

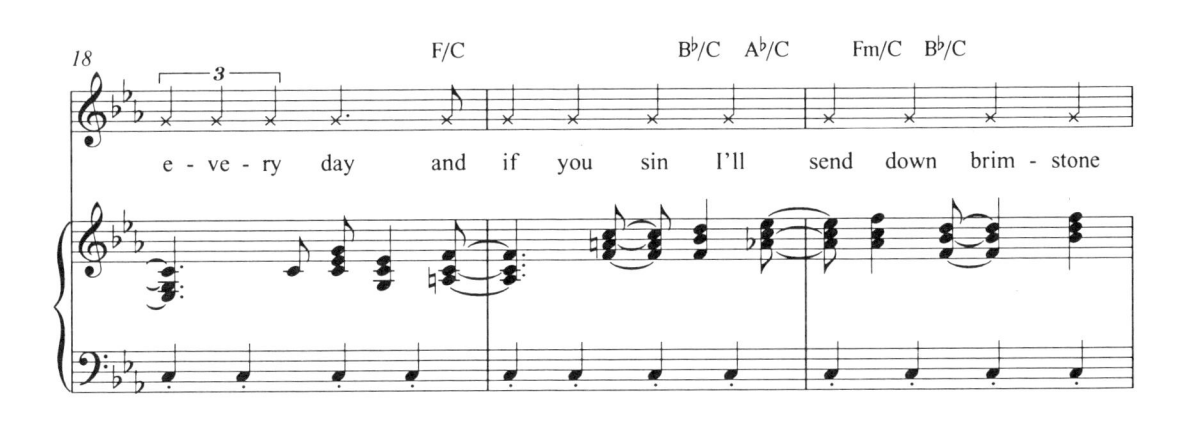

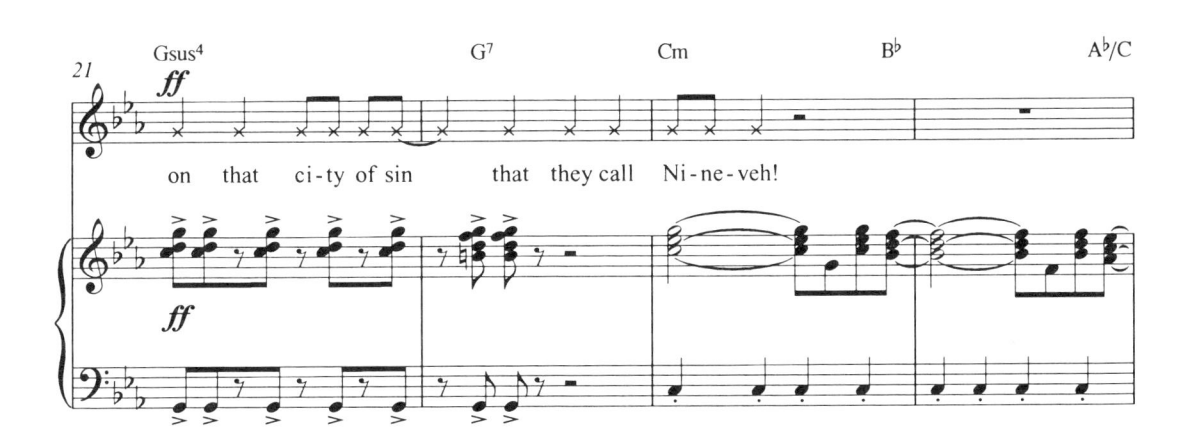

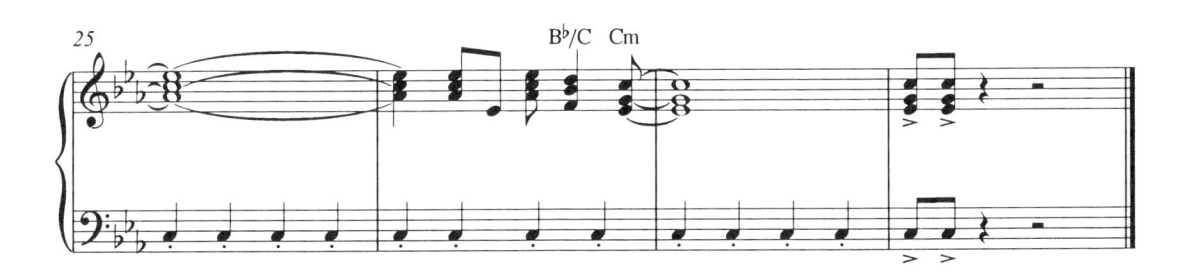

I shall give you this last warning, I will watch you every day and if you sin I'll send down brimstone on that city of sin that they call Nineveh!

17. GOD'S AVENGING PROPHET

Jonah returns, still breathing fire and brimstone, only to be told that God has forgiven the Ninevites and the city's destruction is cancelled. Jonah, far from pleased, stalks away to sit outside the city.

Powerfully (♩ = 160)

Jonah

Now you've had it! That's your lot, I've wait-ed far too long! You've sunk so low in sin and vice you can't tell right from wrong. Come on, Yah-weh, zap 'em now! And give 'em all you've got. Let's show this un-re-pen-tant mob your ven-geance is red hot!

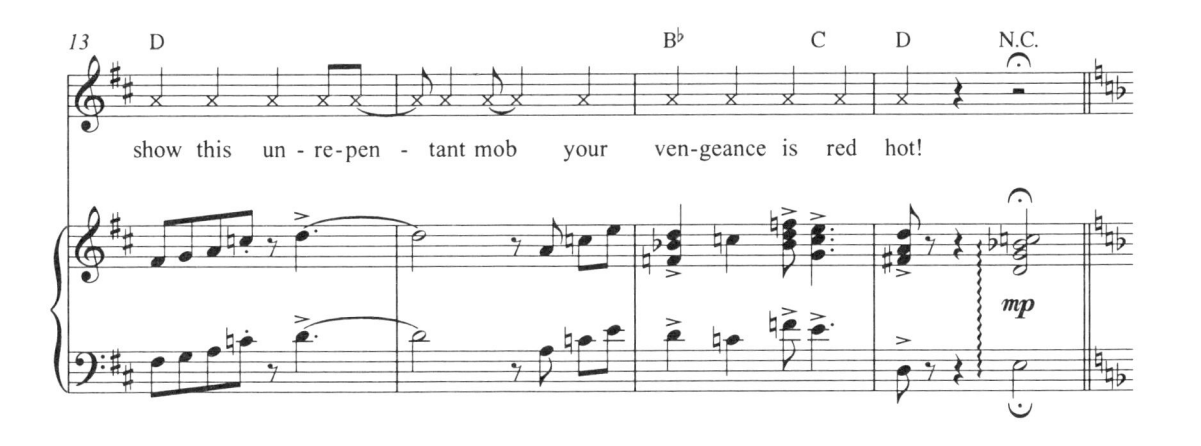

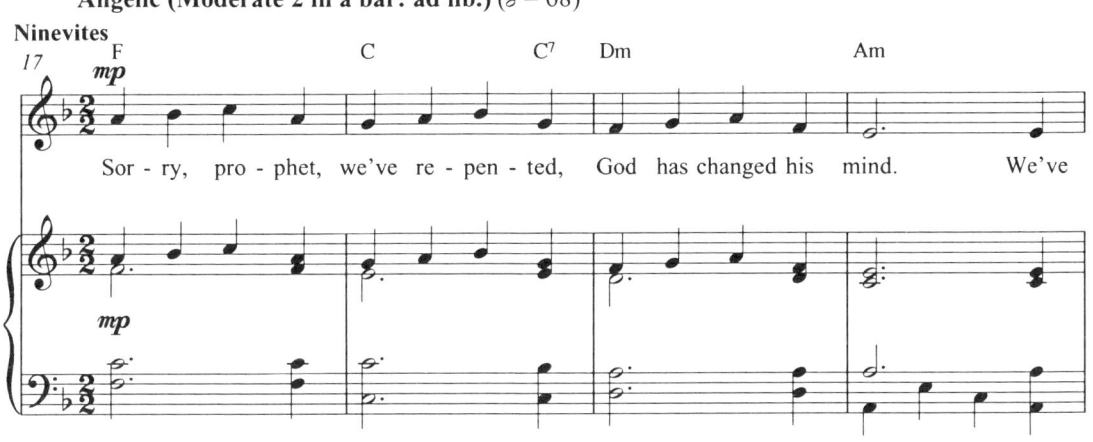

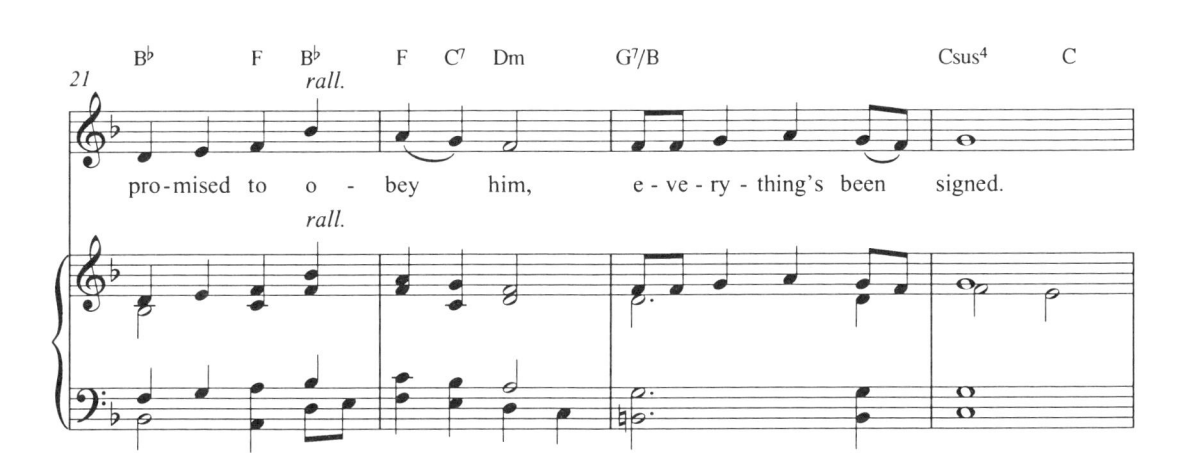

Angelic (Moderate 2 in a bar: ad lib.) ($\quarter = 68$)

Ninevites

Sor-ry, pro-phet, we've re-pen-ted, God has changed his mind. We've pro-mised to o-bey him, e-ve-ry-thing's been signed.

We agreed to change our ways if God called off your show, you
could have been a megastar — but now we'll never know, never know.

18. THE COOL IVY TREE

God provides an ivy tree for Jonah's shelter. The trees take part in a graceful dance as they shield Jonah with their branches. The worms enter and nibble the foliage, killing the tree. The peevish prophet is not pleased!

Easy Latin feel (♩ = 122)

mp sustained

Ivy Trees *mp gently, consoling*

Come, lone - ly Jo - nah   and rest   for a while,   you've been through
Look, gen - tle Jo - nah,   just see   what he's done.   Now we can't

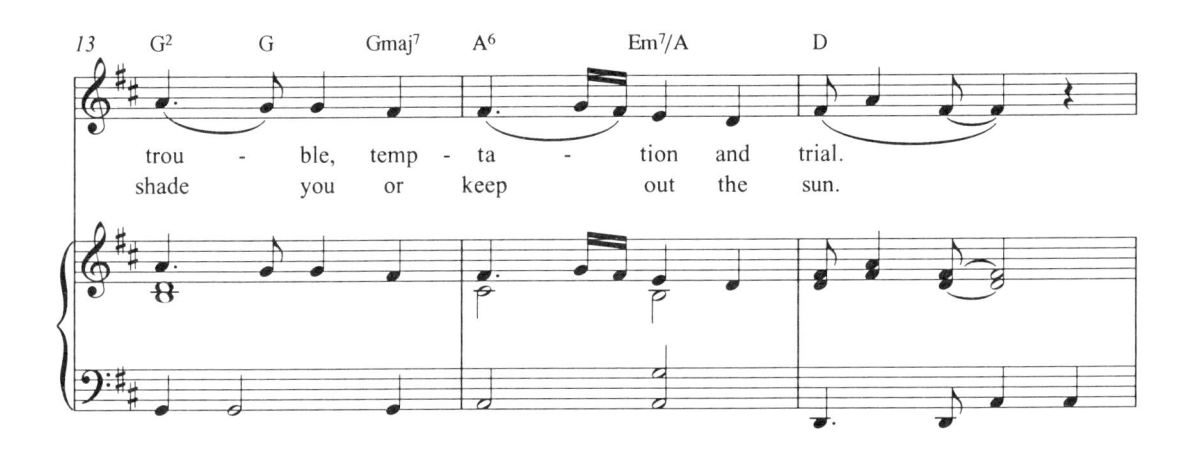

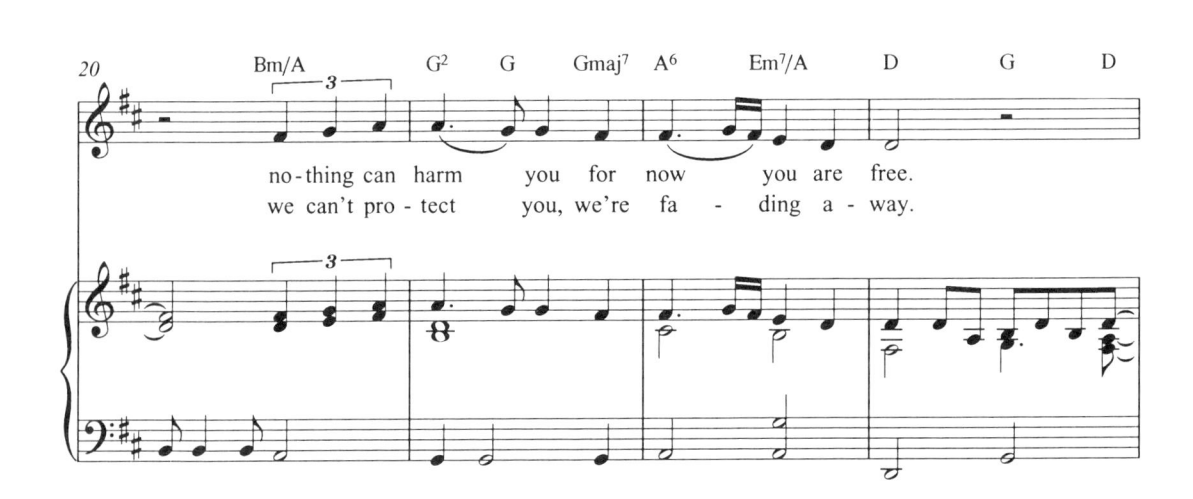

trou - ble, tempt - ta - tion and trial.
shade you or keep out the sun.

Rest from your la - bours, look up and see:
Hear that Si - roc - co com - ing this way,

no-thing can harm you for now you are free.
we can't pro - tect you, we're fa - ding a - way.

Ivy Trees 1
N.C.
G6
G
mf
Just like a sai - lor when he reach - es the
Let's come to - ge - ther and we'll all ga - ther
Ivy Trees 2
mf
Just like a sai - lor
Let's come to - ge - ther
F♯m7
G
Gmaj7
har - bour we'll be your ref - uge, an
round him, stretch out our branch - es and
when he reach - es the har - bour
and we'll all ga - ther round him,
A6
A7
D
D/F♯
e - ver - green ar - bour. Rest on the
try to sur - round him. Dream on and
e - ver - green ar - bour,
try to sur - round him.

33

sil - ver sand, you are safe here with us, ly - ing peace-ful - ly
when you wake and the storm has passed by, look a - round and see,

the sil - ver sand, ly - ing peace-ful - ly
and when you wake, look a - round and see,

36

in the shade of the cool i - vy,
what is left of the cool i - vy,

in the shade of the cool i - vy,
what is left of the cool i - vy,

39

shade of the cool i - vy, shade of the
left of the cool i - vy, left of the

shade of the cool i - vy, shade of the
left of the cool i - vy, left of the

cool i-vy tree.
cool i-vy tree.
cool i-vy tree.
cool i-vy tree.

Moderate rock tempo ($\quarternote = 126$)

Worm: Cri-key! What a love-ly, jui-cy i-vy tree! All those tas-ty branch-es wait-ing there for me. Thank you, God, I'm grate-ful, what a feast I've got!

52 A — *f*

I shall fill my plate full, then I'll eat the lot! I

54 E⁷ *marcato* — D⁷ — Guitar plays piano melody

knew that you liked 'spar-rers' and was sad to see 'em fall, but

f marcato

56

did-n't know you cared for lit-tle worms like me at all. So I go-

58 A **All Worms**

munch, munch, nib-ble, nib-ble, nib-ble. Munch, munch, nib-

61
D7
- ble, nib-ble, nib-ble. Munch, munch, nib - ble, nib-ble, nib-ble.
64
A
E7
marcato
Munch, munch, nib - ble, nib-ble, nib-ble. I - vy, I've a - dored you from the
marcato
67
D7
Guitar plays melody
ff
mo-ment that I saw you, I go – munch, munch, I want you for lunch!
ff
70
A
A7
Guitar plays melody

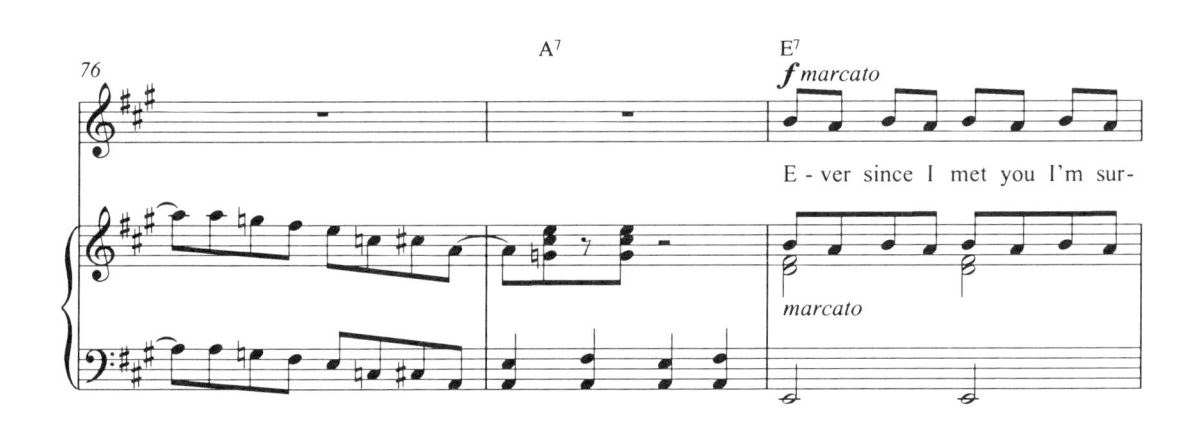

E - ver since I met you I'm sur- prised that no one's ate you, I go – munch, munch, I want you for lunch!

19. JONAH, STOP THAT SULKING

God enlightens Jonah about the irony of his concern for a short-lived tree when he reproaches God for sparing a whole city.

Forbearing (♩ = 140)

God spoken: rhythm ad lib.

Jo - nah, stop that sulk-ing, it was just an i - vy tree. It was-n't your cre - a - tion so you can't get mad with me. If you real - ly loved my peo - ple and looked at things my way you'd be glad I spared those sin-ners down in the ci-ty of sin that they call

Attacca

20. HEY, JONAH!

Jonah is acclaimed for his eventual obedience and his successful mission to Nineveh as everybody celebrates.

Celebratory ($\quarternote = 130$)

God Ni-ne-veh!

f bright and rhythmic

All: Group 1
Hey, hey, hey, hey, hey, Jo-nah!

All: Group 2
Hey, hey, hey, hey, hey, Jo-nah!

5
7
B♭
Hey, hey, hey, hey, hey, Jo - nah! Come back here,
Can't you see
Hey, hey, hey, hey, hey, Jo - nah!
9
E♭
can't you see
what we mean?
Come back here, can't you see
Can't you see what we mean?

what a ce - le - bra - tion there's gon - na be? Here on earth
You're the great - est pro - phet there's e - ver been. So re - joice,

gon - na be?
e - ver been.

sempre staccato

and a - bove
ce - le - brate,

Here on earth
So re - joice

and a - bove.
ce - le - brate.

now you've turned our hat - red to love. Oh, Jo - nah, you've taught
ev - 'ry - bo - dy thinks you're just great! Oh, Jo - nah, you've saved

Oh, Jo - nah, you've taught
Oh, Jo - nah, you've saved

us to change our ways,
us from sin and shame,

us to change our ways, our ways,
us from sin and shame, and shame,

Nineveh is singing your praise. Oh, Jonah, when God
ev-'ry-bo-dy's singing your name. Oh, Jonah, how hap-

Nineveh is singing your praise. Oh, Jonah, when God
ev-'ry-bo-dy's singing your name. Oh, Jonah, how hap-

looked around he knew,
-py and glad we are,

looked around he knew, he knew
-py and glad we are, we are,

23   F   B♭   N.C.   **1.**   *(Back to p. 104)*

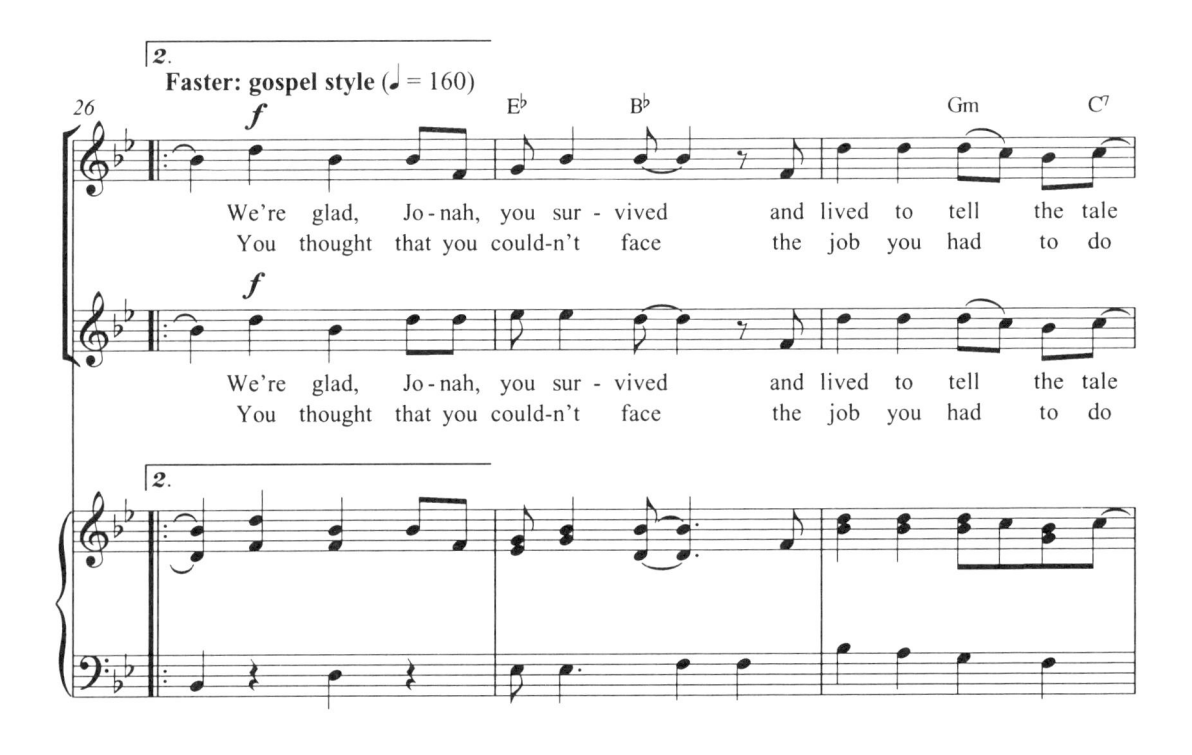

no one could have done it but you!
God has made you in - to a star!

no one could have done it but you!
God has made you in - to a star!

2. **Faster: gospel style** (♩ = 160)

26   *f*   E♭   B♭   Gm   C⁷

We're glad, Jo-nah, you sur - vived and lived to tell the tale
You thought that you could-n't face the job you had to do

f

We're glad, Jo-nah, you sur - vived and lived to tell the tale
You thought that you could-n't face the job you had to do

110

29

Lyrics line 1: of how you sat for three whole days in-side the bel-ly of a whale.
Lyrics line 2: but in the end you came up trumps, they can't take that a-way from you!
Backing: Oo doop doop b' doop doop doop doop doop doop in-

(1.) a whale.

35
Jo-nah, oh, Jo-nah, you'll al-ways be re-

38
C7 F7 B♭ B♭7
mem-bered for sure. Your chan-ces were ze - ro but you
mem-bered for sure. Doop doop b' doop doop doop
40
E♭ Gdim B♭/F C7/G F7 Gm
end-ed up a he - ro, we'll sing your praise for e-ver - more.
doop doop doop we'll sing your praise for e-ver - more.
42
E♭m6 E♭m B♭/F E♭maj7/F F
molto rall.
Yes, we'll sing your praise for e - ver -
Yes, we'll sing your praise for e - ver -
molto rall.

Expansive: not too slow (♩ = 128)
45
ff
B♭
A♭6
E♭
more! Sing - ing your prai - ses for e - ver-
47
B♭
A♭6
E♭
B♭
rall. al fine
A♭6
more! Sing-ing your prai - ses for e - ver- more! Sing-ing your prai-
50
E♭
B♭
- ses for e - ver - more!

> For permission to copy the following eleven pages of text please complete the photocopying licence form at the back of the book.

JONAH!

Text and Lyrics: Denis O'Gorman
Music: Barry Hart

1. JONAH, CAN YOU HEAR ME?

God
(spoken) Jonah! Jonah!
Jonah, can you hear me?
Have you got me loud and clear?
Jonah, are you listening?
Because I'm looking down from here.
I can see the people scorning
every single thing I say,
I have caught them
doing things I could not mention
down in the city of sin that they call *Nineveh!
(*Pronounced Ninn-uh-veh)

Jonah
Yes, God, I can hear you
speaking from the cloud.
But, Lord, I implore you
please don't shout so loud.   **Choir**
I agree the things that you see   Aah
must make you really mad,
the deeds they do must anger you,
Jonah/Choir
I must admit that things are looking bad.

God
(spoken) Jonah! Jonah!
Jonah, I'm not finished,
I've got something more to say.
Jonah, if they keep on sinning
I swear I'll wipe them all away!
Now my anger's really blazing!
Jonah, you must not delay.
Hurry up for
you must preach of my intention
down in the city of sin that they call Nineveh!

Jonah
Yes, God, I am with you,
just rely on me.
Yes, Lord, I'm your servant
as I'm sure you see.   **Choir**
Now I know that I've got to go   Aah
to preach in Nineveh
and tell them straight it's not too late,

Jonah/Choir
I promise, Lord, I'm leaving right away.

Jonah   **Choir**
I'm not afraid to go there   Yes, God, I am
I'll show them, come what may.   with you.
I'm gonna be great,
Lord, I can't wait, I'm leaving
Jonah/Choir
right away, etc.

2. WAIT A MINUTE, JONAH

Little Devils 1
Wait a minute, Jonah,
Little Devils 2
Wait, wait, wait a minute.
Little Devils 1
just before you go,
Little Devils 2
Just, just, just before you go.
Little Devils 1
don't you think there's one more thing
Little Devils 2
Don't, don't, don't you think?
Little Devils 1
that you ought to know?
Little Devils 2
That, that, that you ought to know?
Little Devils 1
Nineveh's a big, bad city,
there's a punch up every night
and they'll have your guts for garters
if you get in a fight.

God will stop at nothing to get his way.
You're a fool to trust him so get away.
Don't delay.

Think about it, Jonah,
Little Devils 2
Think, think, think about it.
Little Devils 1
don't get taken in,
Little Devils 2
Don't, don't, don't get taken in.

Little Devils 1
what's it got to do with you
Little Devils 2
What's, what's, what's it got?
Little Devils 1
if they wanna sin?
Little Devils 2
If, if, if they wanna sin?
Little Devils 1
Can't you see this deal's one-sided.
What your sacrifice will cost?
So get smart, buzz off and scarper,
run away and get lost.
Buzz off and scarper,
sling your hook and get lost!
Buzz off and scarper,
on your bike and get lost!
And get lost!

3. BY JOVE! YOU'RE RIGHT

Jonah
By Jove!
Little Devils / Choir
By Jove!
Jonah
You're right,
Little Devils / Choir
We're right
Jonah
I'm not
Little Devils / Choir
you're not
Jonah / Little Devils / Choir
a Ninevite.
Jonah
I daren't
Little Devils / Choir
You daren't
Jonah
go there
Little Devils / Choir
go there
Jonah / Little Devils / Choir
and get into a fight.
Jonah
I won't
Little Devils / Choir
You won't
Jonah
obey
Little Devils / Choir
obey

Jonah
or go
Little Devils / Choir
or go
Jonah / Little Devils / Choir
to Nineveh.
Jonah
I'm scared
Little Devils / Choir
You're scared
Jonah
to death,
Little Devils / Choir
to death,
Jonah / Little Devils / Choir
I'd / you'd better run away.

Jonah
How I wish my Momma could be here
to tell me what to do –
Momma
Jonah!
Come back home at once,
I'm flaming mad with you!

Jonah
It's just
Little Devils / Choir
It's just
Jonah
not fair
Little Devils / Choir
not fair
Jonah
of God
Little Devils / Choir
of God
Jonah / Little Devils / Choir
to send me / you there,
Jonah
if I
Little Devils / Choir
if you
Jonah
get caught
Little Devils / Choir
get caught
Jonah / Little Devils / Choir
I / you wouldn't have a prayer
Jonah
I'd soon
Little Devils / Choir
You'd soon

Jonah
be dead
Little Devils / Choir
be dead
Jonah
for they'd
Little Devils / Choir
for they'd
Jonah / Little Devils / Choir
cut off my / your head.
Jonah
If God's
Little Devils / Choir
If God's
Jonah
so brave
Little Devils / Choir
so brave
Jonah / Little Devils / Choir
then he can go instead.

Jonah
I'm sure that Momma would approve,
she always knows what's best –
Momma
Jonah!
I could box your ears,
you bloomin' little pest!

Jonah
So now
Little Devils / Choir
So now
Jonah
I'll slip
Little Devils / Choir
you'll slip
Jonah
away
Little Devils / Choir
away
Jonah / Little Devils / Choir
and catch a ship,
Jonah
it's time
Little Devils / Choir
it's time
Jonah
to go

Little Devils / Choir
to go

Jonah / Little Devils / Choir
and take a little trip.

Jonah
I heard
Little Devils / Choir
You heard
Jonah
them say
Little Devils / Choir
them say
Jonah
they sail
Little Devils / Choir
they sail
Jonah / Little Devils / Choir
from Joppa Bay,
Jonah
I must
Little Devils / Choir
you must
Jonah
go there
Little Devils / Choir
go there
Jonah /Little Devils / Choir
and try to get away,
Jonah
away,
Little Devils / Choir
away,
Jonah
away,
Jonah / Little Devils / Choir
and try to get away!
Hey!

4. JONAH, I CAN SEE YOU

God *(spoken)*
Jonah, I can see you running
but you won't get very far.
Jonah, don't you think you've lost me,
because I know just where you are.
Now I'm out to get you, Jonah,
I won't let you get away,
I'll make you
go and do what I command you
down in the city of sin that they call Nineveh!

5. EVERYBODY'S WELCOME TO JOPPA

Holiday-makers
Sunshine and sand
and the Joppa Town Band,
it's lovely to be back here once more!
All
Once more!
Holiday-makers
Down by the sea
eating chips on the quay
and watching all the boats on the shore. **Choir**
Licking pink candyfloss, La, la,
sending postcards to the boss, la, la, la.
Workers
'Sir, we miss you, wish you were here.'
Holiday-makers
We're having fun getting tanned in the sun
and fishing off the end of the pier.

Children / Choir
The funfair is teeming
with spotty kids screaming,
Spotty Kids
'I wanna big Cheeseburger Whopper!'
Children / Choir
They're selling choc ices
at scandalous prices,
kebabs on a stick,
it's no wonder they're sick,
All
so, everybody's welcome to Joppa!

Holiday-makers
What a great sight,
there's pop music all night
that plays non-stop from midnight till four.
All
Till four!
Holiday-makers
Ev'ryone knows
that the pubs never close,
you couldn't ask for anything more. **Choir**
All the clubs here have blokes La, la
telling very funny jokes, la, la la.
Comedian
'Nudge, nudge, wink, wink, know what I mean?'
Holiday-makers
Then you can go to a star-studded show
or crowning of the carnival queen.
Children / Choir
You'll find this amusing,
your granny is losing
at bingo and no one can stop her.
She can't stand the tension,
Granny
'I've just blown me pension!'
Children / Choir
But never you mind,
they look out for her kind
All
'cause everybody's welcome to Joppa!

Sailors
Who wants a trip
on our luxury ship?
We're sailing off to Tarshish today.
All
Today!
Sailors
Come, ev'ryone,
if you wanna have fun,
we're waiting here to take you away.

Captain **Sailors**
And the ship's in good shape, La, la,
she's been twice around the Cape – la, la.
Captain / Sailors
rest assured she's safe as a ship can be.
If you feel bored we can take you aboard,
we're sailing at a quarter to three.

All
Hey, you must be joking,
your fuel tanks are smoking,
Solo
that engine will soon come a cropper!
All
You'll never make Tarshish,
we don't need new glasses
to see that your boat
won't be able to float
and ev'rybody's safer in Joppa!

Jonah
Hey, here take my suitcase,
I'm fed up with this place,
that sounds like a very good offer.
All
You must be a nutter
to sail on that cutter,
still we can all see
if you drown in the sea
you're better off than living in Joppa!

All
La, la, la, etc.
We can't make you notice
how clapped out that boat is,
still if you must go
we shall say, *(shouted)* 'Cheerio!'
So arrivederci from,
arrivederci from,
arrivederci from Joppa!
Bon voyage!

6. THE STORM SEQUENCE

Sailors
Hear that thunder,
Ashur's angry,
Negal's hoppin' mad.
Ishtar's fuming,
Adad's raging;
things are looking bad.
Mighty gods, we've got the message,
can't you tone it down?
We beg you Shammash,
Nego, Nushka, Marduk, please
(shouted) we don't wanna drown!

They won't answer,
nothing's happened,
they don't wanna know!

Captain
Chuck the cargo,
drop the anchor,
clear the decks below.
Sailors
Okay, Captain, let's get moving,
leave the gods alone.
It's clear that
we must ride this storm without them 'cause
(shouted) now we're on our own!

Solo 1
The gods are angry
and someone round here's to blame.
We better pick straws
'cause we gotta find out his name.
Sailors
Hey you! What you doing, stranger?
Wake up! We are all in danger,
so you better join in too –
'cause it might be you.

Solo 2
I've picked a long straw,
nobody can blame me.
Solo 3
And mine is the same,
take a look for yourself and see.
Sailors
Okay, stranger, now it's your go.
Come on, open up your hand so
ev'ryone can see if it is . . .

Solo 1 / Sailors
Wow! It's you, you're the one to blame! **Sailors**
You might as well confess. Oo,
It's not our gods, it's yours, you know, doop. . .
who went and got us in this mess!
Sailors
this mess!
Solo 1 / Sailors
Your God sure is mad with you **Sailors**
and got you on the run, Oo,
so spill the beans, start talking now doop. . .
and tell us what it is you've done!

Tell us, now tell us,
why did you have to leave home and run? **Sailors**
You've been up to something doop. . .
'cause he didn't do this for nothing
so tell us what it is you've done,
just you tell us what it is you've done!

Jonah
I am a Hebrew Jonah,
I should be in Nineveh.
In a dream I heard God calling,

Jonah / Choir
'Jonah, do not delay.'
I knew I couldn't face them,
so I disobeyed the Lord.
If you want to calm this tempest,
throw me in the sea and leave me.
Throw me, it's the truth, believe me.
Throw me overboard!

Sailors
Cool it, Jonah,
we won't harm you,
we won't let you die.
Now you've told us,
we are certain
you're an honest guy.

Maybe God will let us row
another mile or two.
We beg you
God, you saved the ark of Noah, Lord
(*shouted*) come and save us too.

Jonah
No! Throw me in the sea!
Sailors
Row!
Jonah
No! Can't I make you see?
Sailors
Row!
Jonah
No! I've betrayed the Lord!
Sailors
Row!
Jonah
No! Throw me overboard!
Sailors
Then go, go, go, go, go, go, go, go, Go!

7. BYE, BYE, JONAH

Solo Sailor
So it's bye, bye, Jonah, bye, bye,
All Sailors
Oo, Oo.
Solo
What a sporting fellow, a really good guy.
All Sailors
We're so sad you have to leave us,
it's true, please believe us,
Solo   **Sailors**
we could sit down and cry –   boo, hoo
All Sailors
so now it's bye, bye, Jonah,
Solo
Jonah, bye, bye.

8. UNDERWATER DANCE SEQUENCE

God (*shouted*)
Jonah!

9. JONAH, LOOK AROUND YOU

God (*shouted*)
Jonah! Jonah!
Jonah, look around you,
I hope you're wet and cold.

Now I'm going to teach you
to do what you've been told!
Though I've calmed the sea above you,
believe me I'm not through,
I'm sending a gigantic whale
and, Jonah, I will make it swallow you!

[Instrumental]

Jonah, just you stay there
for now you're in disgrace.
You'll find it most unpleasant
in that dark and smelly place.
Maybe that will teach you
that I always get my way.
I've locked you up inside a whale
and that's where you will stay.

10. YAHWEH, PLEASE DON'T LEAVE ME

Jonah
Yahweh, please don't leave me,
broken and in pain;
Father, please believe me
we could start again.
Master, can you hear me?
Are you still out there?
Tell me you're still near me
in this hour of my dark despair.

Lonely and forsaken,
now at last I see
that the path I've taken
couldn't set me free.
Lord, I disobeyed you,
thought I'd be all right;
now God, please show mercy
on your servant down here tonight.

Sea Creatures / Choir
Jonah,
have no fear,
though you have fallen far down here.
Jonah,
don't despair,
surely the Lord has heard your prayer,
calling you back from death's dark night
into the morning light.

Jonah / Sea Creatures / Choir
Father, you still love me,
I can see the light

shining up above me,
everything's all right.
I can feel the sunshine,
I can see the sky,
I know it's a sure sign
that you won't leave me here to die.

Jonah
I shall rise again.
Sea Creatures / Choir
Yes, God, I am with you,
Jonah
I shall rise again.
Sea Creatures / Choir
yes, God, I am with you,
Jonah
I shall rise again.
Sea Creatures / Choir
yes, God, I am with you,
Jonah
I shall rise
Jonah / Sea Creatures / Choir
again.

11. SIN CITY

Ninevites / Choir
Rockin' round the streets of Sin City,
baby, better hold on tight.
Come on, let your hair down,
see what's cookin' down town,
we could have a ball tonight.
So let's sing as we swing
to the beat of the music,
shakin' as we twist and jive.
Stay beside me, honey,
watch me spend m' money,
Nineveh is comin' alive!
(*shouted*) Yeah!

Ninevites / Choir / Little Devils
Rockin', rollin', baby, can't you see
you could have a good time,
rockin' round with me?
Honey, won't you put your hand in mine?
You send shivers down my spine!
When I'm with you ev'rythin's all right,
babe, you drive me crazy
when you hold me tight.
Anything you want now, just let me know,
come on and let yourself go!

Ninevites / Choir
Rockin' round the streets of Sin City,
we'll go boppin' all night long.
All the city's ravin', happy misbehavin',
groovin' as we're movin' along.
Ev'ryone havin' fun givin' wild, crazy parties,
this could really blow your mind.
Baby, don't you leave me, sugar, please believe me,
ev'rythin' is gonna be fine!
(*shouted*) Yeah!

Ninevites / Choir / Little Devils
Rockin', rollin', baby, can't you see
you could have a good time,
rockin' round with me?
Honey, won't you put your hand in mine?
You send shivers down my spine!
When I'm with you ev'rythin's all right,
babe, you drive me crazy
when you hold me tight.
Anything you want now, just let me know,
come on and let yourself go!

Oo, doo wop b'doo di doo . . .
aah
yeah!

Rockin', rollin', baby, can't you see
you could have a good time,
rockin' round with me?
Honey, won't you put your hand in mine?
You send shivers down my spine!
When I'm with you ev'rythin's all right,
babe, you drive me crazy
when you hold me tight.
Anything you want now, just let me know,
come on and let yourself go!
Anything you want now, just let me know.

Ninevites / Choir
Come on!
Little Devils
(*shouted*) Come on!
Ninevites / Choir
And let!
Little Devils
(*shouted*) And let!
Ninevites / Choir
Come on!
Little Devils
(*shouted*) Come on!
Ninevites / Choir

And let!
Little Devils
(shouted) And let!
Ninevites / Choir
Come on and let yourself go!
Go! Go! Go!
Come on, pretty baby, won't y' let yourself go!
Yeah!

12. REPENT!

Jonah
Idolators! Repent!
You sinful, wicked men.
You've offended Yahweh
but you won't do that again.
You'll be shaking like a leaf
when you hear what's in store.
For heathen, pagan scum like you
will burn! burn! burn! for evermore!

13. BYE, BYE, JONAH

High Priest
Oo, just look, what have we here?
What a funny little chap!
So bold, so brave and so sincere,
you've fallen in our lap.
You came here to cause a fuss,
to preach on sin and vice.
Instead you've come and given us –
a perfect sacrifice!

Ninevites / Choir
Mighty Negal, here's your dinner,
how d'you want him done?
As a spicy burger
in a double-decker bun?
Would you like him toasted, roasted,
quite well done or rare?
We could stew him, barbecue him,
anytime or anywhere.
Or would you like him cut in slices,
boiled with cook-in sauce?
Tarted up with lots of spices
for your second course?
Take your time, you needn't hurry,
we could mince and stir
what's left over in a curry,
simply say what you prefer.

Ninevites / Choir / Handmaidens
So it's bye, bye, Jonah, bye, bye,
Oo, oo.
Negal wants his dinner, so now you must die.
'Cause when strangers come to meet 'im,
he just wants to eat 'em,
boiled or baked in a pie –
so now it's bye, bye, Jonah,
Jonah, bye, bye.

Doo, doo, doo, doo . . .
High Priest
Negal's getting thinner
so he needs a bigger dinner like you.
Ninevites / Choir / Handmaidens
Doo, doo, doo, doo . . .
High Priest
Negal says he's starving
so we better start with carving up you.

Ninevites / Choir / Handmaidens
Doo, doo, doo, doo . . .
High Priest
We must do what Negal wishes,
serve you up on silver dishes
and you'll really taste delicious in a stew!

Ninevites / Choir / Handmaidens
Doo, doo, doo, doo . . .
High Priest
Negal's tum is rumbling
so we gotta stop him grumbling right now.
Ninevites / Choir / Handmaidens
Doo, doo, doo, doo . . .
High Priest
Now we got the venue
we must work out Negal's menu somehow.
Ninevites / Choir / Handmaidens
Doo, doo, doo, doo . . .
High Priest
He could have your nose for starters,
eat your toes with fried 'tomarters',
then your legs with chipolatas right now!

Ninevites / Choir / Handmaidens
So it's bye, bye, Jonah, bye, bye,
Oo, oo.
Negal wants his dinner, so now you must die.
'Cause when strangers come to meet 'im,
he just wants to eat 'em,
boiled or baked in a pie –
so now it's bye, bye, Jonah,
bye, bye, Jonah,

bye, bye, Jonah,
Jonah, bye, bye,
Jonah, bye, bye,
Jonah, bye, bye,
ciao!

14. GOD'S AVENGING PROPHET

Jonah
Don't you touch me!
One more step
and you'll go up in flames!
I am God's avenging prophet
sent to take your names.
One by one
he'll punish you
and no one can resist.
Just one step,
I'm warning you,
and you'll be on my list!

Start repenting,
on your knees,
you'd better hear me through.
After watching all your sinning,
God is mad with you.
Change your ways
or he will send
a plague upon your town,
then return in forty days
and burn, burn, burn, your city down!

15. SHOW HIM YOU'RE REPENTING

King
Now you've blown it,
I should have known it,
I can't let you out of my sight.
Now you've dropped us in it,
we've got one minute,
if we're gonna put things right.   **N-vites / Choir**
Grab some hairshirts,   Aah.
start repenting!
Put on ashes,
start lamenting!
King / Ninevites / Choir
Get that hair cut off your head;
King   **N-vites / Choir**
show him you're repenting.   We're sorry,
                                      didn't mean to
                                      do it!
Show him you're repenting.   We're sorry,
                                      didn't mean to
                                      do it!

King
Now I've seen it,
I know he means it,
this guy wants to see us all dead.
But God might show pity
and save our city,
if we do the things he said.

Ninevites / Choir
Call on Yahweh,   Aah.
kneel before him.
Raise your hands high
and adore him,
King / Ninevites / Choir
show this prophet you have changed;
King   **N/vites / Choir**
show him you're repenting.   We're sorry,
                                      didn't mean to
                                      do it!
Show him you're repenting.   We're sorry,
                                      didn't mean to
                                      do it!

[Instrumental]

King   **N-vites / Choir**
Call on Yahweh,   Aah.
kneel before him.
Raise your hands high
and adore him,
King / Ninevites / Choir
show this prophet you have changed;
King   **N-vites / Choir**
show him you're repenting.   We're sorry,
                                      didn't mean to
                                      do it!
Show him you're repenting.   We're sorry,
                                      didn't mean to
                                      do it!

King
Show him you're repenting.
Ninevites / Choir
Show him you're repenting.
Show him you're repenting!

16. YOUR CITY WILL BE SAVED

God *(spoken)*
All right now, that's enough,
I can see your heads are shaved.
You're looking quite repentant
so your city will be saved.
I shall give you this last warning,
I will watch you every day,

and if you sin I'll send down brimstone
on that city of sin that they call Nineveh!

17. GOD'S AVENGING PROPHET

Jonah
Now you've had it! That's your lot,
I've waited far too long!
You've sunk so low in sin and vice
you can't tell right from wrong.
Come on, Yahwah, zap 'em now!
And give 'em all you've got.
Let's show this unrepentant mob
your vengeance is red hot!

Ninevites
Sorry, prophet, we've repented,
God has changed his mind.
We've promised to obey him,
everything's been signed.
We agreed to change our ways
if God called off your show,
you could have been a megastar –
but now we'll never know,
never know.

18. THE COOL IVY TREE

Ivy Trees
Come, lonely Jonah
and rest for a while,
you've been through trouble,
temptation and trial.
Rest from your labours,
look up and see:
nothing can harm you
for now you are free.

Ivy Trees 1
Just like a sailor
Ivy Trees 2
Just like a sailor
Ivy Trees 1
when he reaches the harbour
Ivy Trees 2
when he reaches the harbour
Ivy Trees 1
we'll be your refuge,
an evergreen arbour,
Ivy Trees 2
evergreen arbour.
Ivy Trees 1
Rest on the silver sand,
Ivy Trees 2
the silver sand,
Ivy Trees 1
you are safe here with us,
Ivy Trees 1 & 2
lying peacefully
in the shade of the cool ivy,
shade of the cool ivy,
shade of the cool ivy tree.

Worm
Crikey! What a lovely, juicy ivy tree!
All those tasty branches waiting there for me.
Thank you, God, I'm grateful,
what a feast I've got!
I shall fill my plate full,
then I'll eat the lot!
I knew that you liked 'sparrers'
and was sad to see 'em fall,
but didn't know you cared
for little worms like me at all.
So I go –

Worms
Munch, munch, nibble, nibble, nibble.
Munch, munch, nibble, nibble, nibble.
Munch, munch, nibble, nibble, nibble.
Munch, munch, nibble, nibble, nibble.
Ivy, I've adored you
from the moment that I saw you,
I go –
munch, munch,
I want you for lunch!

[Instrumental]

Ever since I met you
I'm surprised that no one's ate you,
I go –
munch, munch,
I want you for lunch!

Ivy Trees
Look, gentle, Jonah,
just see what he's done.
Now we can't shade you
or keep out the sun.
Hear that Sirocco
coming this way,
we can't protect you,
we're fading away.

Ivy Trees 1
Let's come together
Ivy Trees 2
let's come together
Ivy Trees 1
and we'll all gather round him,
Ivy Trees 2
and we'll all gather round him,
Ivy Trees 1
stretch out our branches
and try to surround him,
Ivy Trees 2
try to surround him.
Ivy Trees 1
Dream on and when you wake,
Ivy Trees 2
and when you wake,
Ivy Trees 1
and the storm has passed by,
Ivy Trees 1 & 2
look around and see,
what is left of the cool ivy,
left of the cool ivy,
left of the cool ivy tree.

19. JONAH, STOP THAT SULKING

God *(spoken)*
Jonah, stop that sulking,
it was just an ivy tree.
It wasn't your creation
and so you can't get mad with me.
If you really loved my people
and looked at things my way
you'd be glad I spared those sinners
down in the city of sin that they call Nineveh!

20. HEY, JONAH!

All: Groups 1 & 2
Hey, hey, hey, hey, hey, Jonah!
Hey, hey, hey, hey, hey, Jonah!
Come back here, can't you see
what a celebration there's gonna be?
Here on earth and above
now you've turned our hatred to love.
Oh, Jonah, you've taught us to change our ways,
Nineveh is singing your praise.
Oh, Jonah, when God looked around he knew,
no one could have done it but you!
Hey, hey, hey, hey, hey, Jonah!
Hey, hey, hey, hey, hey, Jonah!

Can't you see what we mean?
You're the greatest prophet there's ever been.
So rejoice, celebrate,
ev'rybody thinks you're just great!
Oh, Jonah, you saved us from sin and shame,
ev'rybody's singing your name.
Oh, Jonah, how happy and glad we are,
God has made you into a star!

We're glad, Jonah, you survived
and lived to tell the tale   Oo, doop . . .
of how you sat
for three whole days
inside the belly of a whale,   a whale.
You thought that you couldn't face
the job you had to do   Oo, doop . . .
but in the end you came up trumps,
they can't take that away from you!

Jonah, oh, Jonah,
you'll always be remembered for sure.
Your chances were zero   doop . . .
but you ended up a hero,
we'll sing your praise for evermore.
Yes, we'll sing your praise for evermore!
Singing your praises for evermore!
Singing your praises for evermore!
Singing your praises for evermore!

Please photocopy this page

KEVIN MAYHEW PERFORMANCE AND PHOTOCOPYING LICENCE FORM

We are delighted that you are considering *Jonah!* for production.
Please note that a performance licence is required and royalties are payable as follows:

10% of gross takings, plus VAT
(Minimum fee: £25.00 + VAT = £29.37)

This form should be returned to the Copyright Department at Kevin Mayhew Ltd. A copy, including our performance licence number, will be returned to you.

Name of Organisation _____

Contact name _____

Contact address _____

_____

Postcode _____

Contact Telephone No. _____ Contact Fax No. _____

E-mail _____

Date(s) of performance(s) _____

Venue _____

Seating capacity _____

Proposed ticket price _____

Please tick:

☐ I am not charging admission for my performance.
   I enclose the minimum fee.

☐ I am charging admission and undertake to submit performance fees due to Kevin Mayhew Ltd. within 28 days of the last performance, together with a statement of gross takings.

☐ I require a words-only photocopying licence and enclose £5.85 (inc.VAT).

Signature _____

Name (please print) _____

On behalf of _____

Address if different from above _____

_____

To be completed by Kevin Mayhew Copyright Department:

Performance/Photocopying Licence No _____

is issued to _____ For _____ performance(s)

of _____ on _____

Signed _____ for Kevin Mayhew Ltd.   Date _____

Copyright Department, Kevin Mayhew Ltd, Buxhall, Stowmarket, Suffolk, IP14 3BW
Telephone number: UK 01449 737978   International +44 1449 737978
Fax number: UK 01449 737834   International +44 1449 737834
E-mail: copyright@kevinmayhewltd.com